The Whole Grain Cookbook

Arto der Haroutunian is now a British citizen but was born in Aleppo, Syria in 1940. His father's family were from Southern Turkey and his mother's from Armenia. He took a degree in architecture at Manchester University and has been a practising architect ever since, specializing in designing restaurants, clubs and hotels.

In 1970, in partnership with his brother, he opened the first Armenian restaurant in Manchester, which has developed today into a successful chain of restaurants and hotels. As well as his passion for cooking Arto der Haroutunian is a painter of international reputation who has exhibited all over the world. His other interests include composing music and translating Turkish, Arab, Persian and Armenian authors. He lives in Cheshire with his wife and son.

His books *Middle Eastern Cookery* and *The Barbecue Cookbook* are also available in Pan.

D0550511

Other cookery books available in Pan

Mrs Beaton's Cookery for All
Carol Bowen **The Microwave Cookbook The Food Processor Cookbook**
Arto der Haroutunian **Middle Eastern Cookery The Barbeque Cookbook**
Gail Duff's Vegetarian Cookbook
Theodora FitzGibbon **Crockery Pot Cooking Irish Traditional Food**
A Taste of . . . series
Michel Guérard's Cuisine Minceur
Kenneth Lo **Quick and Easy Chinese Cooking Healthy Chinese Cooking**
Claire Loewenfeld and Philippa Back **Herbs for Health and Cookery**
Maurice Messegue and Madeleine Peter **A Kitchen Herbal**
Elizabeth Orsini **The Book of Pies**
Margaret Paterson **1001 Ways to be a Good Cook**
Marguerite Patten **Learning to Cook**
Roger Phillips **Wild Food**
V. V. Pokhlebkin **Russian Delight**
Evelyn Rose **The Complete International Jewish Cookbook**
Katie Stewart **Shortcut Cookbook The Times Calendar Cookbook**
The Times Cookery Book Katie Stewart's Cookbook
Rita Springer **Caribbean Cookbook**
Marika Hanbury Tenison's Freezer Cookbook

The Whole Grain Cookbook

Arto der Haroutunian

Illustrated by Marilyn Day

Pan Books London and Sydney

First published 1987 by Pan Books Ltd,
Cavaye Place, London SW10 9PG
9 8 7 6 5 4 3 2 1
© Arto der Haroutunian 1987
Illustrations © Marilyn Day 1987
ISBN 0 330 29958 1

Phototypeset by Rowland Phototypesetting Ltd,
Bury St Edmunds, Suffolk
Printed by Cox and Wyman Ltd,
Reading, Berks

Contents

Introduction

'Crush not yon ant, who stores the golden grains,
He lives with pleasure and will die with pain;
Learn from him rather to secure the spoils,
Of patient cares and preserving toils'

Saidi

Some of the finest dishes from every culinary tradition in the
world are those which are based on grains. In combination with
ingredients such as meat or fish, vegetables, fruit or nuts, they
provide dishes which are richly satisfying and highly nutritious.

The history of cereal grains is the history of mankind's
transition from a nomadic to a sedentary life. All the world's
ancient civilisations were based on grains. Those in the Middle
East (Egypt, Sumer, Asia Minor), and thence Europe, were
founded on wheat and barley. In the Far East it was rice that
became the mainstay of Chinese, Indian and Japanese
cultures. In the Americas it was maize and in Africa, sorghum
and millet.

Food patterns that developed thousands of years ago have
remained very consistent. In China and Japan rice is still the
staple diet. In Africa it is still sorghum, while in Mexico maize
still predominates.

Cereal grains have been used in numerous ways. They can
be cracked or coarsely ground, or turned into flour for
bread-making. Grains also act as raw material for the
preparation of beer, alcohol, starch, and as concentrated feed
for farm animals. Furthermore the products of grain
processing are used in baking, macaroni, cous-cous, polenta
and the confectionery industries (Appendix 1). In ages gone by
grain was either roasted or boiled in water or milk and then
consumed as porridge. In time other ingredients were added to
this bowl of porridge to enrich its flavour, add substance and,
no doubt, to create variety. Grains are deficient in some
amino-acids (see Appendix 2), but the addition of other
ingredients such as pulses, nuts, vegetables etc. helps produce
a much more harmonious dietary balance.

Thus was created one of the greatest foods of all – the pilav
(pilao, pollo, risotto, paella, kasha), a form of cooking where
grain is cooked with herbs, spices, vegetables, nuts, fruits,

meat, poultry and fish. Pilav dishes are prepared with whole grains. The most important ones are rice, wheat, cracked wheat, buckwheat, rye, millet and maize. There are, of course other grains such as oats, sorghum, triticale (foxtail, barnyard, turkestan) millets, green bristle grass etc. These, however are not readily available to us and, in some cases not suitable for the preparation of pilav dishes.

There are also a few non-cereals such as sago, tapioca, soya, cous-cous, polenta, semolina etc. which are the milled products of grains or pulses.

This book then is about whole grain *pilavs*. I have not included any recipe dealing with whole grains in soups, stews, desserts or drinks.

A few words about grains

A grain of cereal grass is a dry, monospermous fruit that is globulous in wheat, rye, corn and the naked forms of barley and turnicate (covered with flowering husks) in oats, barley, rice and millet.

Most cereal grains have an indigestible 'husk' or 'hull' around them which is removed before they are used as human food. The exceptions to this rule are maize, rye and wheat; these are called naked or free-threshing grains. Whole grains are unrefined, thus retaining all the nutritional value of the bran and germ.

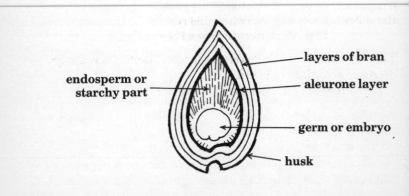

The germ (the embryo of the future plant) contains a great deal of fat, protein, sugar, vitamins and enzymes.

The fibre contained in the outside layers helps to prevent cancer of the colon, gall bladder ailments and, according to some scientists, heart disease.

The endosperm is the heaviest part of the grain from which the most valuable part of flour is obtained during milling.

The outermost layer of the endosperm – the aleurone layer – is rich in proteins and fat (see Appendix 3).

Apart from their nutritional and health advantages, we must bear in mind a third important fact, namely that grains cost less to grow – and hence to purchase – than meats, fish or eggs. In monetary terms alone the spread and wider use of grains would help a fairer and cheaper distribution of food for all.

The cereals used in this book are rice, cracked wheat (burghul), whole wheat grains, buckwheat, barley, millet and rye. A brief history of each grain is given under the appropriate section.

We close our brief introduction to whole grains with a few lines by the Russian poet Apollon Maikov exuding the beauty, brilliance and bountifulness of grain.

SUMMER RAIN
'Gold! it is gold falling down from the sky!'
Children cry, rushing with joy in the rain.
'Nay, but we'll gather gold soon from the plain –
Grain it will be, golden, sweet-swelling grain –
Barns flowing over with ripe wheat and rye!'
Three Centuries of Russian Poetry

The salt content in all the recipes is to my taste. Increase or decrease according to yours.

All recipes are for 6 people unless otherwise specified.

Rice

By far the most widespread and popular grain is rice, which is the staple food of over half the world's population. In Chinese 'to have a meal' ('ch'in fan') literally means 'to eat rice'. It is their 'King of Foods'.

The origins of rice are wrapped in myth and fantasy. This is the story of rice:

'Long, long ago man had no rice with which to still the pangs of hunger, but had to live from fruits and the flesh of wild beasts. It is true that the rice plant was there, but at this time the ears were empty, and naturally no food could be had from them.

One day the goddess Kuari Yin saw how difficult men's lives were and how they were always hungry. Her compassionate heart was touched, and she decided to help them. One evening she secretly slipped down to the fields and pressed her breast with one hand until her milk flowed into the ears of rice. She squeezed until there was no milk left, but all the ears were not yet filled; so she pressed once more with all her might, and a mixture of blood and milk came out . . .

From that time the ears were filled, and man had rice to eat. The white grains are those that were made from her milk, and the ruddy red ones are those that were formed out of the mixture of her milk and blood.'

Chinese Fairy Tales and Folk Tales

Rice was first cultivated over 5,000 years ago in China. The sowing of the first rice was part of a major religious ceremony. The Emperor planted the first seeds, followed by other members of his family.

From China, rice spread to the neighbouring lands of India, Japan and, in time, most of Asia. It is claimed that Alexander the Great brought the rice grain to Europe, but there is no proof of this. Rice is not mentioned in the Old or New Testaments. It is not mentioned in the Koran. Indeed, it only appeared in the Middle East via the Arab conquest of Iran, some thousand years ago, and with the advance of Islam it penetrated Spain, Southern Europe and, in time, Europe generally. Interestingly, the cultivation of rice appears to have spread throughout Asia and Africa mainly through the religions of Buddhism and Islam. Centuries later the Spanish introduced it to the New World, where it soon spread so much so that today the USA is one of the major rice-exporting countries in the world.

There are over 10,000 varieties of rice, but they all fall into the following categories:

a) long-grain
b) medium-grain
c) short-grain
d) glutinous

Long-grain – by far the best is 'Basmati'. This comes from the foothills of the Himalayas. It is aged for one year before appearing in the shops. 'Patna' is an American polished long-grain rice.

Medium-grain – the most popular rice used in Britain is labelled 'Carolina rice'. It is of good consistency, but lacks flavour and absorbs a little more liquid in cooking.

The Italian medium-grain rices, e.g. Arvorio, Cristelio and Arborio, are excellent for risottos, paellas and stuffings. They are also ideal for dishes where the pilav is moulded.

Short-grain – this rice absorbs the most liquid and cooks into a creamy mass. It is excellent for puddings, for the Japanese 'Gohan' and the Chinese 'Congee' dishes.

Glutinous – Of a creamy, opaque colour, this is shorter and rounder than the average long-grain rice. It is very popular in Japan and other South-East Asian countries where the criterion is that the rice should be able to be scooped up with chopsticks – and not eaten with a fork.

In recent years two other types of rice have become popular.

Wild Rice (zizania aquatica) – is a tall aquatic grass and a distant relative of cultivated rice. It grows naturally in Japan, China and parts of North America. Wild rice has long dark brown, needle-thin grains with a distinctive taste. It is very expensive, since to date all attempts to cultivate it commercially have failed. Therefore it is only sold in specialist shops. It is excellent in savoury dishes. It takes about 45 minutes to cook and requires approximately 3 times the volume of water to rice.

Brown Rice – this is simply unpolished rice and consequently it has a higher vitamin B content, a particular flavour of its own and a firmer texture than the white, polished grain.

Below is a basic recipe for brown rice which can be substituted for the standard long-grain rice I have used throughout this book. Simply make sure you adjust the amount of water and the cooking time.

2 tablespoons butter
350g (12oz) brown rice, rinsed thoroughly under cold water and drained
1 teaspoon salt
800ml (1⅓ pints) boiling water or stock

1 Melt the butter in a large saucepan, add the rice and fry for a few minutes, stirring frequently. Add the salt and water or stock and boil vigorously for 1 minute. Lower the heat, cover the pan and simmer for 40–45 minutes. After 30 minutes check and see if the rice seems dry. If it does add a little more boiling water, but do not stir.
2 When cooked, remove from the heat and leave to 'rest' for 10 minutes, before serving.

'Wash your face, your hands, wash your feet, but never wash rice because rice is not proud.'

Italian proverb

Italians may or may not wash their rice, but I suggest from the outset that you wash yours thoroughly for several minutes under cold, running water until the water runs clear.

Plain Rice Pilavs

There are several ways of preparing a plain rice pilav and the following are some of the more popular ones. A general rule, however, is to use 400ml (13fl oz) liquid for the first 175g (6oz) rice and 300ml (10fl oz) for every following 175g (6oz). This rule can be simplified even further for it is easier to cook rice by volume, therefore allow 2 cups of water for the first cup of rice and 1½ cups of water for each preceding cup of rice.

The simplest method of rice cooking is the following which is popular throughout East Asia, China, Korea and Japan.

Heen pahb – Korean white rice

350g (12oz) short-grain rice, rinsed thoroughly under cold running
  water
500ml (16fl oz) water

1 Place the rice in a saucepan, add the water, cover the pan and bring to the boil.
2 Reduce the heat to low and simmer for 30 minutes. Do not remove the lid or stir the rice.
3 Remove from the heat, fluff up with a long-pronged fork and serve as required.

Cheng fan – steamed rice

350g (12oz) short- or long-grain rice, rinsed thoroughly under cold,
  running water
500ml (16fl oz) water

1 Place the rice in a saucepan with the water and leave to soak for 30 minutes.
2 Place the pan on a medium heat and bring to the boil. Reduce the heat to low and simmer, uncovered, for 20 minutes or until all the water has been absorbed.
3 Remove the pan from the heat and transfer the rice to the top of a steamer. Cover and place over boiling water for 20 minutes.
4 Fluff up with a long-pronged fork and serve immediately.

K'ao fan – baked rice

350g (12oz) long-grain rice, rinsed thoroughly under cold, running
  water
500ml (16fl oz) water

1 Place the rice in an ovenproof casserole with the water and leave to soak for 30 minutes.

2 Cover the pan and place in the centre of an oven preheated to 350°F, 180°C, Gas Mark 4 for 40 minutes.
3 Reduce the heat to 275°F, 140°C, Gas Mark 1 and cook for a further 10 minutes.
4 Remove from the oven and serve.

Roz – Arab-style rice

This is a standard recipe used throughout the Middle East. Ghee can be purchased from most Indian grocers.

50g (2oz) butter or ghee
350g (12oz) long-grain rice, rinsed thoroughly under cold, running water
720ml (24fl oz) boiling water
1 teaspoon salt

1 Melt the butter or ghee in a medium saucepan. Add the rice and fry, stirring frequently, for 2–3 minutes.
2 Pour in the boiling water, add the salt and stir. Allow the mixture to boil vigorously for 3 minutes, then cover the pan, lower the heat as far as possible and simmer for about 20 minutes or until all the liquid has been absorbed. The grains should be tender and separate and there should be small holes in the surface of the pilav.
3 Turn off the heat and leave the rice 'to rest' for at least 10 minutes.
4 Carefully fluff up the rice with a long-pronged fork and serve.

Chelo – Iranian plain rice

This is the classic rice pilav of Iran and is often served with a raw egg yolk and a pat of butter.

350g (12oz) long-grain rice, washed thoroughly under cold, running water
2 tablespoons salt
1.65l (2¾ pints) water
50g (2oz) butter, melted

1 Place the rice in a large saucepan, add half the salt and enough cold water to cover it by 2.5cm (1"). Leave to soak for 2 hours.

2 Bring 1.5l (2½ pints) of the water to the boil in a heavy saucepan with a close-fitting lid. Drain the rice thoroughly in a sieve, then pour it slowly into the boiling water and add the remaining salt. Stir it a few times and then boil, uncovered, for 5 minutes.

3 Drain the rice into a sieve. Pour the remaining 150ml (¼ pint) water and half the melted butter into the saucepan; add the rice. Pour the remaining butter over the top.

4 Cover the pan with a tea towel, then fit the lid on and lift the ends of the cloth onto the lid so that there is no danger of them burning. Steam the rice over a very low heat for about 25–30 minutes until the grains have become tender and the liquid has been absorbed.

5 The traditional way of serving this pilav is to place a pat of butter and a raw egg yolk on top of each individual portion and sprinkle with sumac. The whole lot is then mixed together and usually eaten with a spoon.

Ch'ao fan – Chinese fried rice

This is the simplest and the most popular of all Chinese fried rice dishes; very easy to prepare and perfect with any meat, poultry or fish dish. Both soy sauce and peanut oil are available in all major supermarkets and, of course, in Chinese emporiums.

350g (12oz) long-grain rice, washed thoroughly under cold water and drained
1 tablespoon salt
4 teaspoons peanut oil
3 teaspoons soy sauce

1 Half fill a large saucepan with water and bring to the boil. Add the salt and drained rice and boil for 10 minutes.

2 Remove the pan from the heat, drain the rice and leave to cool for 15 minutes.

3 Meanwhile heat the peanut oil over a moderate heat in a large frying pan or in a wok. Add the rice and stir with a wooden spoon until each grain is well coated with oil.
4 Raise the heat, add the soy sauce and fry the rice for 5–6 minutes, stirring constantly. Lower the heat and continue frying and stirring until the rice is moist and tender.
5 Serve immediately.

Rice with Herbs, Spices, Pasta, Eggs and Cheese

'Thunder will not strike one when eating rice'
Chinese proverb

Rice goes brilliantly with herbs and spices. Dill, sumac, saffron, curry powder, fenugreek etc. not only give the grains flavour, but also colour and texture. Rice, like an artist's white canvas, can be skilfully decorated, coloured and patterned.

The first recipe is from Iran, where all housewives are expected to be as skilled in pilav cooking as in carpet weaving!

Sabzi pollo – herb rice

This dish should be prepared with fresh herbs, but since not all these are readily available in Britain I reluctantly suggest that you substitute those unavailable with their dried version.

350g (12oz) long-grain rice, washed thoroughly under cold water and
   drained
1¼ tablespoons salt
50g (2oz) butter
4 tablespoons chopped fresh dillweed OR 2 tablespoons dried dillweed
3 tablespoons chopped fresh fenugreek OR 1 teaspoon dried fenugreek
4 tablespoons chopped parsley
4 tablespoons chopped fresh coriander
4 tablespoons chopped fresh tarragon OR 2 tablespoons dried tarragon
4 spring onions, green parts only, finely chopped

1 Bring about 1.8l (3 pints) water to the boil in a large saucepan. Add the rice and salt and stir. Boil for 10 minutes, then strain into a colander. Rinse the rice with cold water and leave to drain.

2 Melt the butter in a medium-sized saucepan and add one third of the rice. Spread it out evenly and sprinkle half of the chopped herbs and all the spring onions over the surface. Add another third of the rice and top with the remaining herbs. Layer the remaining rice evenly over the top.

3 Cover the pan with a tea towel and then with a tightly fitting lid, lifting the ends of the towel well away from the heat. Place the pan over a very low heat and steam for about 30 minutes.

4 Remove from the heat and leave 'to rest' for about 10 minutes before serving.

Kesari chaval – saffron pilav

Saffron is widely used in rice pilavs, particularly in India, Pakistan and Iran. In the Middle East it is often replaced, for economic reasons, by turmeric. The simplest saffron pilav has ½ teaspoon powdered saffron added to the rice while it is frying. Iranians and Indians often add other spices to their saffron pilav as illustrated below with this Indian recipe which is similar to the Iranian 'Zaffran Pollo'.

½ teaspoon saffron powder OR ¾ teaspoon saffron strands
75g (3oz) ghee or clarified butter
5cm (2″) piece cinnamon stick
6 cloves
2 large onions, thinly sliced
350g (12oz) long-grain rice, washed thoroughly under cold water and drained
720ml (24fl oz) boiling water
1½ teaspoons salt
4 cardamom pods, bruised

1 Put the saffron in a small bowl, add 2 tablespoons boiling water and set aside for 10–15 minutes.

2 Meanwhile melt the ghee or butter in a large saucepan and

add the cinnamon stick, cloves and onions. Fry for about 10
minutes or until the onions are soft, stirring frequently.
3 Add the rice and fry for a further 4–5 minutes, still stirring
frequently.
4 Stir in the water, salt and cardamom pods and boil rapidly
for 2–3 minutes.
5 Reduce the heat to very low and stir in the saffron. Cover the
pan and leave to simmer for 20–25 minutes or until all the
liquid has been absorbed.
6 Leave 'to rest' for 10 minutes and then fluff up with a
long-pronged fork and serve.

Geelryes – yellow pilav

Turmeric gives this pilav its distinctive yellow colouring and
raisins and cinnamon add extra flavour.
   This is a traditional recipe from Northern India and is also
popular in Iran and Afghanistan.

50g (2oz) butter
350g (12oz) long-grain rice, washed thoroughly under cold water and
   drained
1 teaspoon turmeric
1 teaspoon salt
75g (3oz) raisins
5cm (2″) cinnamon stick
2 bay leaves
720ml (24fl oz) boiling water

1 Melt the butter in a medium saucepan, add the rice and fry
for 2–3 minutes, stirring frequently. Add the turmeric, salt,
raisins, cinnamon stick and bay leaves and fry for a few more
minutes, still stirring frequently.
2 Pour in the boiling water and boil vigorously for 2–3
minutes. Lower the heat and simmer for 15–20 minutes or
until all the liquid has been absorbed.
3 Leave the rice 'to rest' for about 10 minutes, fluff up with a
long-pronged fork, discard the cinnamon stick and bay leaves
and serve.

Risotto alla Milanese – Italian saffron pilav

A very popular Italian risotto making use of saffron to enhance its colour. It can be eaten on its own as a savoury, but usually accompanies meat dishes. Some people like to sprinkle the cheese over the top of the pilav rather than mixing it through.

50g (2oz) butter
1 onion, finely chopped
350g (12oz) long-grain rice, washed thoroughly under cold water and drained
120ml (4fl oz) dry white wine
600ml (1 pint) chicken stock, boiling
½ teaspoon saffron threads soaked in 2 tablespoons boiling water
1 teaspoon salt
¼ teaspoon black pepper
75g (3oz) grated parmesan or romano cheese

1 Melt the butter in a medium saucepan. Add the onion and fry until soft.
2 Add the rice and fry for about 5 minutes, stirring frequently.
3 Pour in the wine and half the stock and simmer for 10 minutes, stirring occasionally.
4 Stir in the remaining stock, the saffron mixture, salt and pepper and simmer for a further 10–15 minutes, or until all the liquid has been absorbed.
5 Remove from the heat, stir in the cheese and serve.

Plov azzari – ginger and sesame seed pilav

This recipe, from Azerbaijan in the Southern USSR, is also popular in Northern Iran. It has a fascinating, subtle flavour and is excellent with poultry.

50g (2oz) butter or ghee
350g (12oz) long-grain rice, washed thoroughly under cold water and drained
1 teaspoon ground ginger
1 tablespoon sesame seeds
720ml (24fl oz) chicken stock or water, boiling
1 teaspoon salt
½ teaspoon black pepper

Garnish:
50g (2oz) slivered almonds, toasted

1 Melt the butter in an ovenproof casserole. Add the rice and
fry gently, stirring frequently, for about 10 minutes. Add the
ginger and sesame seeds and fry for a further 2–3 minutes. Stir
in the water or stock, salt and pepper and bring to the boil.
2 Place the casserole, uncovered, in an oven preheated to
350°F, 180°C, Gas Mark 4 for about 35 minutes or until the
water has been absorbed.
3 Turn off the oven and, after 10 minutes, toss the rice with a
fork. Leave in the oven for a further 15–20 minutes and then
toss again.
4 Sprinkle with the almonds and serve.

Shoga meshi – ginger rice

This Japanese way of cooking rice with fresh ginger is also
very popular in neighbouring South-East Asian countries.
Ginger gives a fresh taste to the rice.
   Sometimes kelp (seaweed) is added.

5cm (2″) piece fresh ginger, washed and scraped
350g (12oz) short-grain rice, washed under cold water and drained
540ml (18fl oz) water
2 tablespoons soy sauce
2 tablespoons saké or dry sherry

1 Slice the ginger very thinly, place in a small bowl and soak
in a little water for 30 minutes.
2 Place the rice, water, soy sauce and saké in a saucepan and
bring to the boil.
3 Drain the ginger slices and add to the pan. Cover the pan,
reduce the heat to very low and simmer for about 20 minutes or
until all the water has been absorbed.
4 Remove the pan from the heat, leave to 'rest' for 10 minutes
and then serve.

Nasi uduk – rice with coconut milk and spices

Coconut milk (see Glossary) can be purchased from Indian shops and some large supermarkets. It is used widely in Indonesian cookery, from where this recipe comes.

Petis is thick and grey in colour and is the equivalent of the Chinese 'shrimp paste' which is available in all Chinese food shops. You can substitute anchovy sauce instead.

Serve with duck, chicken, turkey, steaks and chops.

900ml (1½ pints) coconut milk
1½ teaspoons salt
1 medium onion, finely chopped
1 clove garlic, crushed
1 teaspoon cumin
1 teaspoon turmeric
½ teaspoon nutmeg
1½ teaspoons coriander
¼ teaspoon ground cloves
½ teaspoon *petis* or *trasi* (shrimp paste)
1 teaspoon very finely chopped lemon rind
350g (12oz) long-grain rice, washed thoroughly under cold water and
   drained

1 Put all the ingredients, except the rice, in a large saucepan and bring slowly to the boil, stirring frequently with a wooden spoon.
2 Add the rice, mix well, lower the heat, cover the pan and cook for 20 minutes.
3 Uncover the pan and stir the ingredients thoroughly. Replace the lid and cook for a further 5–7 minutes. Serve immediately.

Kari pilav – rice with curry powder

Curry powder gives this simple pilav all the flavour of Northern India. Excellent with fish and shellfish dishes.

50g (2oz) ghee or butter
1 large onion, coarsely chopped
350g (12oz) long-grain rice, washed thoroughly under cold water and
   drained

2 teaspoons curry powder
2–3 cloves
1 teaspoon salt
½ teaspoon garam masala
720ml (24fl oz) boiling water

1 Melt the ghee or butter in a saucepan. Add the onion and fry until soft.
2 Stir in the rice and spices and fry for a further 2–3 minutes.
3 Add the water and bring quickly to the boil. Lower the heat, cover the pan and simmer for about 20 minutes or until the water has been absorbed.
4 Remove from the heat, leave to 'rest' for about 10 minutes and then fluff up with a long-pronged fork and serve.

Şeriyeli pilavi – rice with vermicelli

This is one of the most popular pilavs throughout the Middle East. The recipe below is a typical one. There are, of course, many versions, mostly with additional items such as almonds, pine kernels and spices.

50g (2oz) ghee or butter
50g (2oz) vermicelli, broken into 2.5cm (1″) pieces
350g (12oz) long-grain rice, washed thoroughly under cold water and drained
3 tablespoons raisins (optional)
1 teaspoon salt
720ml (24fl oz) boiling water

1 Melt the ghee or butter in a saucepan. Add the vermicelli and fry until golden, stirring frequently. Stir in the rice, raisins and salt and fry for a further 2–3 minutes.
2 Pour in the water and bring quickly to the boil. Lower the heat, cover the pan and simmer for about 20 minutes or until all the water has been absorbed.
3 Turn off the heat and leave the rice to 'rest' for 10 minutes. Fluff up gently with a long-pronged fork and serve.

Variations: There is no reason why other pastas such as egg noodles, macaroni, tagliatelli, tortellini etc. should not be cooked with the rice as described above. You need not fry the pasta first, but it does look more attractive and also tends to be less 'doughy' if sautéed a little.

Kazmag pilav – rice and dough pilav

'It is the crust which sticks to the rice, not the rice to the crust.' – The poor cling to the rich, not the rich to the poor. (*Chinese proverb*)

A kazmag is a thin, round layer of dough and in this recipe the rice is cooked on this layer of dough.

This is a traditional pilav from the Caucasus and is also popular in Northern Iran.

The pomegranate seeds give this dish a most attractive appearance.

1 egg
salt
75g (3oz) plain flour
2.4l (4 pints) water
¼ teaspoon powdered saffron
350g (12oz) long-grain rice, washed thoroughly under cold water and
  drained
100g (4oz) butter, melted

Garnish:
1 large, ripe pomegranate

1 Break the egg into a mixing bowl and beat until frothy. Add a pinch of salt. Sift in 50g (2oz) of the flour and mix until smooth. Add the remaining flour, a little at a time, and knead until the dough is smooth and does not stick to the fingers.
2 Lightly flour a work top and roll out the dough. Place an ovenproof casserole, about 25cm (10″) in diameter, on the dough and cut around it so that you have a piece of dough which will fit into the base of the casserole. Set the dough aside.
3 Place the water in a large saucepan with the saffron and 1 tablespoon of salt. Bring to the boil. Slowly add the rice so as not to disturb the boiling. Boil briskly for 10 minutes, then drain the rice into a colander.

4 Brush the base of the casserole with a little oil and place the kazmag in the bottom. Brush this liberally with some of the melted butter. Add the rice to the casserole and spread out evenly. Sprinkle with the remaining butter.
5 Cover the casserole with a tea towel and then a lid. Cook over a very low heat for 35–40 minutes.
6 To serve, pile the rice onto a large plate and garnish with wedges of the golden-brown kazmag crust. Peel the pomegranate and sprinkle the seeds over the rice.

Egg and rice pilav

A filling, savoury dish of rice with hard-boiled eggs in a curry sauce. It is cheap and easy to prepare and very tasty with a bowl of fresh salad.

50g (2oz) butter
350g (12oz) long-grain rice, washed thoroughly under cold water and
  drained
1 teaspoon salt
720ml (24fl oz) boiling water
50g (2oz) butter
1 onion, finely chopped
3 tablespoons plain flour
1½ tablespoons curry powder
½ teaspoon salt
½ teaspoon paprika
½ teaspoon turmeric
600ml (1 pint) milk
9 hard-boiled eggs, shelled and halved lengthways

Topping:
4 tablespoons breadcrumbs
1 tablespoon coarsely chopped almonds
1 tablespoon butter

1 First prepare the rice by melting 50g (2oz) of the butter in a saucepan. Add the rice and fry for a few minutes, stirring frequently. Stir in the salt and water and bring quickly to the boil. Lower the heat, cover the pan and simmer until all the water has been absorbed. Set aside.

2 To prepare the sauce melt 50g (2oz) of butter in a small pan.
Add the onion and fry until soft. Stir in the flour, curry powder,
salt, paprika and turmeric and cook for a further 2 minutes.
Add a little milk at a time, stirring constantly, until you have
a thick, smooth sauce.

3 Grease a large casserole about 25–30cm (10″–12″) in
diameter and 7.5cm (3″) deep.

4 Spoon the cooked rice into the casserole. Spread some of the
rice out over the base and push the rest up around the sides to
form a mould about 5cm (2″) deep. Press the rice together so
that it holds firm.

5 Arrange the halved eggs, cut sides down over the base and
then pour the sauce into the centre to cover the eggs.

6 Mix the breadcrumbs and almonds together and sprinkle
over the top. Dot the surface with butter and bake in an oven
preheated to 350°F, 180°C, Gas Mark 4, for about 20 minutes or
until the top is lightly browned.

7 Remove from the oven and serve immediately.

Plov shashandaz – omelette pilav

A delightful recipe from Azerbaijan. It can be eaten as a
savoury or served with kebabs and roasts.

Do be generous with the cinnamon, it gives the pilav extra
flavour and new dimensions.

Pilav:
50g (2oz) butter
½ teaspoon saffron dissolved in 2 tablespoons boiling water
1 teaspoon salt
350g (12oz) long-grain rice, washed thoroughly under cold water and
  drained
720ml (24fl oz) boiling water

Omelette:
50g (2oz) butter
1 large onion, finely chopped
1½ tablespoons lemon juice
1 teaspoon sugar

6 eggs
1 teaspoon salt

Garnish:
50g (2oz) melted butter
1 teaspoon cinnamon

1 First prepare the pilav by melting the butter in a saucepan.
Add the diluted saffron, salt and rice and fry for a few minutes,
stirring frequently. Add the water and bring to the boil.
2 Lower the heat, cover the pan and simmer until all the
water has been absorbed.
3 Set aside 'to rest' while the omelette is prepared.
4 Melt the butter in a large frying pan; add the onion and fry,
stirring occasionally, until it is golden. Stir in the lemon juice
and sugar.
5 Beat the eggs in a mixing bowl with the salt until they are
frothy. Pour the egg mixture over the onion and let it spread
out evenly. Reduce the heat to very low and leave the omelette
to cook without disturbing it.
6 When the centre is beginning to firm, invert a plate over the
pan and turn the omelette over onto the plate. Slide the
omelette back into the pan to cook on the other side until
golden.
7 Remove the omelette from the pan and roll it up as you
would a pancake. Shred it across the roll into 1cm (½″) strips.
8 To serve pile the rice onto a serving platter and garnish it
with the omelette strips. Dribble the butter over the top and
sprinkle with the cinnamon.

Banirov pilav – cheese pilav

An Armenian speciality. Feta or Haloumi cheese are usually
used, but Cheddar or Cheshire will do very well instead.

50g (2oz) butter
250g (9oz) long-grain rice, washed thoroughly under cold water and
  drained
600ml (1 pint) boiling water
1 teaspoon salt

175g (6oz) brown or white breadcrumbs
175g (6oz) grated cheese – Feta, Haloumi, Cheddar or Cheshire

Garnish:
15g (½oz) butter
25g (1oz) blanched almonds
25g (1oz) pine kernels
½ teaspoon sumac powder

1 First prepare the rice by melting the butter in a saucepan. Add the rice and fry for a few minutes, stirring frequently. Stir in the water and salt and bring quickly to the boil. Lower the heat, cover the pan and simmer for about 20 minutes or until all the water has been absorbed.
2 Set aside to 'rest' for 10 minutes.
3 Lightly grease a shallow, ovenproof dish about 20–22.5cm (8″–9″) in diameter. Add half the rice, spreading it evenly over the base. Spread half the breadcrumbs over the rice, then half the cheese over the breadcrumbs.
4 Spread the remaining rice evenly over the layer of cheese, and top with the remaining cheese. Finally sprinkle the remaining breadcrumbs over the top and press down firmly.
5 Place in the centre of an oven preheated to 350°F, 180°C, Gas Mark 4, and bake for about 30 minutes, or until the breadcrumbs are toasted and golden.
6 When ready to serve, make the garnish by melting the butter in a small pan. Add the almonds and pine kernels and fry until golden. Remove with a slotted spoon and sprinkle over the pilav. Sprinkle with the sumac and serve.

Riz au gratin – cheese pilav

A very tasty French pilav. It makes an ideal savoury when served with salads, but it is also served with roast meats.

50g (2oz) butter
250g (9oz) long-grain rice, washed thoroughly under cold water and drained
1 teaspoon salt
600ml (1 pint) boiling water

1 tablespoon butter
1 tablespoon flour
300ml (½ pint) milk
50g (2oz) grated cheese
½ teaspoon salt

Topping:
50g (2oz) breadcrumbs
1 tablespoon butter
25g (1oz) grated Parmesan cheese

1 First prepare the rice by melting the butter in a saucepan.
Add the rice and fry for a few minutes, stirring frequently. Stir
in the salt and water and bring quickly to the boil. Lower the
heat, cover the pan and simmer until all the water has been
absorbed. Set aside while the sauce is prepared.
2 Melt the butter in a small pan and stir in the flour.
Gradually work in the milk, stirring constantly until the sauce
is thick and smooth.
3 Stir in the cooked rice, cheese and salt. Mix well.
4 Lightly grease an ovenproof dish about 20–22.5cm (8″–9″) in
diameter. Turn the rice mixture into the dish and spread out
evenly. Spread the breadcrumbs over the top, dot with the
butter and sprinkle the Parmesan cheese over the top.
5 Cook in an oven preheated to 350°F, 180°C, Gas Mark 4, for
about 20 minutes or until lightly browned.
6 Remove from the oven and serve immediately.

Rice with Vegetables

'I have gathered my rice. I have mended my roof. Blow now winds and
let the cold rain fall.' – *Chinese expression*

Most vegetables go well with rice, whether they are boiled,
baked or fried together. In this chapter we shall be dealing
with rice cooked only with vegetables, usually just one or two.
No meats of any type are included. There is a charming
Chinese expression which goes thus: 'In China we have only

three religions, but we have a hundred dishes we can make from rice.' This adage is adequate to a point. Unfortunately there is often too much 'sameness' amongst those hundred dishes, for the Chinese concept of 'vegetables with rice' basically implies a rice dish which has been impregnated with the *flavour* of a vegetable. This is in contrast to Mediterranean cooking in general where the vegetables vie with the rice for prominence.

I have included a few typical Chinese vegetable-rice recipes. The repertoire is large and you can experiment to your heart's content by using any of the following vegetables and more: mushrooms, peas, watercress, carrots, bamboo shoots, sweetcorn, Chinese cabbage etc.

Ch'ao fan – rice with spring onions

350g (12oz) long-grain rice, washed thoroughly under cold water and drained
600ml (1 pint) water
1 teaspoon salt
2 tablespoons butter
225g (8oz) spring onions, cleaned and then cut into 2cm (1½″) lengths

1 Place all the ingredients in an ovenproof casserole and bring to the boil. Mix thoroughly, cover and place in an oven preheated to 350°F, 180°C, Gas Mark 4. Cook for 15 minutes and then turn off the heat and leave the casserole in the oven for a further 15 minutes.
2 Serve with any Chinese or Japanese dish or with any roast meat.

Chai ch'ao fan – Chinese vegetarian fried rice

This is a glorious dish.

If you wish you can, instead of the vegetables suggested below, use a larger proportion of one vegetable or experiment with others of your choice such as spinach, peas, chopped lettuce etc.

350g (12oz) short-grain rice, washed thoroughly under cold water and
  drained
10 dried Chinese mushrooms
3 tablespoons peanut oil
1 teaspoon finely grated fresh ginger
2–3 spring onions, washed, trimmed and cut into 1cm (½″) pieces
2 cloves garlic, crushed
1 tablespoon sesame oil
2 leeks, trimmed, washed thoroughly and thinly sliced using white
  part and 7.5cm (3″) of the green leaves
2 sticks celery, washed, stringed and thinly sliced diagonally
225g (8oz) green beans, stringed and cut into thin diagonal slices
1 large carrot, scraped and grated
2 tablespoons soy sauce
1½ teaspoons salt

1 Boil the rice in the way described in Ch'ao fan (fried rice)
page 8.
2 Meanwhile soak the mushrooms in 450ml (15fl oz) hot water
for 30 minutes and then squeeze out and reserve as much of the
liquid as possible. Discard the mushroom stems and cut the
caps into thin strips.
3 Heat the peanut oil in a wok or large frying pan on a
moderate heat. Add the ginger, onions, garlic and sesame oil
and fry, stirring constantly, for 30 seconds. Now add the
vegetables, raise the heat and stir-fry for 3 minutes.
4 Add the pre-cooked rice and fry, stirring frequently, until
heated through.
5 Add 120ml (4fl oz) of the reserved mushroom liquid, the soy
sauce and salt and mix thoroughly. Serve immediately.

Kong na-mool pahb – Rice and bean-sprouts

'You cannot buy honourable rice from a dead relation.' – *Korean
proverb*

A Korean dish. Serve with gammon or fish.

1 teaspoon peanut or vegetable oil
2 tablespoons soy sauce
2 spring onions, washed, trimmed and cut into 1cm (½″) pieces

1 clove garlic, thinly sliced
1 tablespoon prepared sesame seeds (see Glossary)
110g (4 oz) bean sprouts (mung or soy), washed
350g (12oz) short-grain rice, washed thoroughly under cold water and
    drained
480ml (16fl oz) water

1 Place the oil, soy sauce, spring onions, garlic, prepared
sesame seeds and beansprouts in a medium-sized saucepan and
cook over a high heat for 2 minutes, stirring constantly with a
wooden spoon.
2 Stir in the rice and water and bring to the boil. Cover the
pan, lower the heat and cook for 25–30 minutes. Serve
immediately.

Lobi-siseri pilav – kidney bean and chickpea pilav

This dish is often eaten as a snack with natural yogurt, but it
also makes an ideal accompaniment to all kebabs and grilled
meats.

75g (3oz) red kidney beans, soaked overnight in cold water
75g (3oz) chickpeas, soaked overnight in cold water
3 tablespoons oil
1 large onion, coarsely chopped
350g (12oz) long-grain rice, washed thoroughly under cold water and
    drained
1 teaspoon salt
½ teaspoon cinnamon
½ teaspoon coriander
1 teaspoon cumin
75g (3oz) flaked almonds or chopped hazelnuts
50g (2oz) raisins
720ml (24fl oz) boiling water

1 Drain the kidney beans and chickpeas. Place them in
separate saucepans and cover generously with cold water.
Bring both pans to the boil, boil for 10 minutes, then lower the
heats and simmer until the beans and peas are tender. Add
more boiling water if necessary.
2 Drain and set aside.

3 Heat the oil in a large saucepan, add the onion and fry until soft, stirring frequently. Add the rice, kidney beans and chickpeas and fry for a further 2–3 minutes.

4 Stir in all the remaining ingredients and bring quickly to the boil. Cover the pan, lower the heat and simmer for about 20 minutes or until all the liquid has evaporated.

5 Set aside to 'rest' for about 10 minutes and then fluff up with a long-pronged fork and serve.

Dampokhtk – broad bean pilav

This is a popular Iranian pilav which is eaten on its own with yoghurt or as an accompaniment to meat dishes.

Although dried broad beans can be used, I strongly recommend the use of fresh beans as they give this pilav a very earthy taste and interesting texture.

50g (2oz) butter
2 medium onions, thinly sliced
2 teaspoons turmeric
350g (12oz) shelled broad beans
720ml (24fl oz) boiling water
1½ teaspoons salt
350g (12oz) long-grain rice, washed thoroughly under cold water and
  drained

To serve:
50g (2oz) butter, melted
Bowl of natural yoghurt

1 Melt the butter in a large saucepan. Add the onions and fry until golden, stirring frequently. Add the turmeric, broad beans and one third of the water, cover and simmer for 5 minutes.

2 Stir in the salt, rice and remaining water, cover and simmer for a further 15–20 minutes or until all the water has evaporated.

3 Remove from the heat, cover the rice with a tea towel and replace the lid. Set aside for 15–20 minutes until the rice is fairly dry.

4 Turn the pilav into a serving dish and dribble the melted butter over it. Serve on its own with a bowl of yoghurt or as an accompaniment to roast or grilled meats.

Adzuki gohan and onigiri – Adzuki bean pilav and rice balls

Adzuki beans, originally from Japan, are now grown extensively throughout Europe and USA and are available at many supermarkets and health food stores.

75g (3oz) adzuki beans, soaked overnight in cold water
250g (9oz) short-grain rice, washed thoroughly under cold water and
  drained
¼ teaspoon salt

1 Drain the beans, place in a saucepan and add enough cold water to cover by about 5–7.5cm (2–3″). Bring to the boil, keep boiling for 10 minutes, then reduce heat to medium-low, cover and simmer for 30–45 minutes or until the beans are just tender. Add a little cold water at least twice during the cooking time. In Japan this is called 'surprise water'. It acts to reduce the cooking time and hasten the softening.
2 When the beans are just tender drain them, but retain 3–4 tablespoons of the cooking water.
3 Return the beans to the saucepan and mix in the rice, salt and reserved bean water. Add 360ml (12fl oz) water and cover the pan. Bring to the boil, reduce heat to low and simmer for 30 minutes. Do not remove the lid or stir the rice.
4 At this stage Adzuki gohan can be served as a pilav or it can be formed into rice 'balls'.
5 There are 4 basic rice 'ball' (onigiri) shapes: round, triangular, spherical and cylindrical.

To prepare the balls take handfuls (about the size of a billiard ball) of the pilav and sculpt into the desired shapes.

6 Apart from the shape there are other ways in which to vary the balls. The contents can be changed e.g. peas, black beans or ginkgo nuts used instead of the adzuki beans and the balls can be wrapped in Nori (seaweed) or lightly coated with Miso (p. 228).

7 The balls can be eaten as they are or can be grilled until the surface is golden and the rice is crisp.

8 Needless to say you can continue to develop this theme by experimenting with the inclusion of pine kernels, raisins, chopped almonds etc.

Hoppin' John – Black-eye bean pilav

A traditional West Indian recipe which is also very popular in the southern states of the USA. There are several versions, but basically the ingredients are black-eye beans, rice and onions. You can also incorporate salt pork and tomatoes.

225g (8oz) black-eye beans, soaked overnight in cold water
250g (9oz) long-grain rice, washed thoroughly under cold water and drained
1 teaspoon salt
25g (1oz) butter or bacon dripping
1 medium onion, finely chopped
450g (1lb) tomatoes, blanched, peeled and chopped
½ teaspoon cayenne pepper
½ teaspoon black pepper

1 Drain the beans and place in a saucepan. Add enough cold water to cover by 7.5cm (3″) and bring to the boil. Boil for 10 minutes, then reduce the heat to medium and simmer for 30 minutes or until the beans are just tender. Add more water if necessary.

2 Drain the beans and reserve 450ml (¾ pint) of the cooking water.

3 Return the beans and reserved liquid to the saucepan and stir in the rice and salt. Bring to the boil, lower the heat and simmer for 10 minutes.

4 Meanwhile melt the fat in a small frying pan and sauté the
onion until soft. Add the tomatoes, cayenne and black pepper,
stir and fry gently until the rice has been cooking for 10
minutes. Then stir this mixture into the bean and rice mixture
and simmer for a further 10–15 minutes or until all the liquid
has been absorbed.
5 Set aside to 'rest' for 10 minutes, fluff up with a long-pronged
fork and serve.

Muddara – lentil and rice pilav

Lentils make marvellously tasty pilavs, as I am sure you will
agree when you have tried this recipe and the following one.

   This is an Arab (Syrian and Lebanese) speciality. This pilav
is usually eaten as a savoury, with a bowl of fresh salad, some
pickles and natural yoghurt. You can substitute bulghur
(cracked wheat) for the rice – the traditional Armenian and
Kurdish method (p. 119).

175g (6oz) whole brown lentils, rinsed and drained
900ml (1½ pints) cold water
200ml (⅓ pint) vegetable or olive oil
2 large onions, thinly sliced
2 teaspoons salt
½ teaspoon black pepper
450ml (¾ pint) boiling water
250g (9oz) long-grain rice, washed thoroughly under cold water and
   drained

1 Put the lentils in a large saucepan, add the water and bring
to the boil. Lower the heat, cover the pan and simmer for about
20–30 minutes, or until the lentils are almost tender and the
water mostly absorbed.
2 Meanwhile heat the oil in a frying pan, add the onions and
fry, stirring frequently until they are a dark golden colour, but
not burnt.
3 When the lentils have been cooking for 20–30 minutes add
half the onions and oil to the pan together with the salt, pepper
and boiling water. Stir in the rice and bring quickly to the boil.

Lower the heat, cover the pan and simmer for 15–20 minutes
or until the rice is tender and the water absorbed.
4 Turn off the heat and leave the pilav to 'rest' for 10 minutes.
5 Pile the muddara onto a plate and garnish with the
remaining onion and oil. Serve with pickles, salad and
yoghurt.

Kitry – Rice and lentil pilav

This is from Iraq, but is also popular in the Gulf States. There
is more than a hint of the Indian sub-continent in this recipe.
Even the name is undoubtedly derived from the classic
'kitcheri'.

150g (4½oz) whole brown lentils, rinsed thoroughly
3 tablespoons oil
2 cloves garlic, finely chopped
2 tablespoons tomato purée
1 teaspoon turmeric
1 teaspoon salt
250g (9oz) long-grain rice, washed thoroughly under cold water and
  drained
600ml (1 pint) boiling water

1 Drain the lentils and place in a saucepan. Add enough cold
water to cover by 5cm (2″) and bring to the boil. Lower the heat
and simmer for 15–20 minutes. Pour the contents of the pan
into a colander and set aside to drain.
2 Heat the oil in a large saucepan and fry the garlic, stirring
occasionally, for 2 minutes. Add the tomato purée, turmeric
and salt and fry for a further 2 minutes.
3 Add the rice and lentils and stir until they are well coated
with the mixture. Add the water and bring to a quick boil.
Lower the heat, cover the pan and simmer until rice and lentils
are tender and water has been absorbed.
4 Set aside to 'rest' for 10 minutes and then serve as an
accompaniment to vegetable and/or meat dishes.

Vegetable kitcheri – Indian rice, lentil and vegetable pilav

Kitcheris are basically a mixture of rice and lentils. There are many variations; some may include other vegetables or pulses, meat or fish.

This vegetable kitcheri makes use of potatoes, carrots, peas, aubergine and tomatoes, but you can add or substitute other favourite vegetables e.g. courgettes, cauliflower, spinach etc.

Serve on its own with yoghurt or as an accompaniment to any meat dish.

110g (4oz) whole brown lentils, rinsed thoroughly
50g (2oz) butter or ghee
1 large onion, thinly sliced
2 green chillis, finely chopped
2 cloves garlic, crushed
2.5cm (1″) piece root ginger, peeled and finely chopped
8 peppercorns
Seeds of 2 cardamom pods
1 bay leaf
½ teaspoon turmeric
110g (4oz) carrots, peeled and cut into 1cm (½″) cubes
110g (4oz) peas
1 small aubergine, cut into 2.5cm (1″) cubes
2 large tomatoes, blanched, peeled and chopped
1½ teaspoons salt
110g (4oz) potato, peeled and cut into 2.5cm (1″) cubes
225g (8oz) long-grain rice, washed thoroughly under cold water and
  drained
50g (2oz) red lentils, rinsed thoroughly
600ml (1 pint) boiling water or stock

1 Put the whole brown lentils in a saucepan and cover by about 2.5cm (1″) with cold water. Bring to the boil and simmer for 15 minutes or until almost tender. Drain and set aside.
2 Meanwhile melt the butter or ghee in a large saucepan and fry the onion until soft, stirring occasionally. Add the green chillis, garlic, ginger, peppercorns, cardamom seeds, bay leaf and turmeric. Fry for a further 2 minutes, stirring constantly.
3 Now add the carrot, peas, aubergine, tomatoes and salt and fry for 5 minutes, stirring occasionally.

4 Add the drained lentils, potato, rice and red lentils and stir well. Pour in the boiling stock or water, mix well, cover the pan, reduce the heat and simmer for 20–30 minutes or until all the liquid has been absorbed.

5 Set aside for a few minutes and then transfer to a large dish and serve.

Harem pilav – Avocado pilav

A Middle Eastern pilav by origin, this recipe makes use of avocados, tomatoes, mushrooms and wine.

  Especially good with poultry and pork dishes.

110g (4oz) butter
1 large onion, finely chopped
1 clove garlic, coarsely chopped
350g (12oz) long-grain rice, washed thoroughly under cold water and
  drained
600ml (1 pint) boiling water
120ml (4fl oz) white wine
2 teaspoons salt
1 teaspoon black pepper
175g (6oz) button mushrooms, wiped clean and halved
6 medium tomatoes, blanched, peeled and chopped
¼ teaspoon dried oregano
1 ripe avocado, peeled and diced

Garnish:
1 tablespoon finely chopped parsley or tarragon

1 The rice for this pilav can be either cooked in the oven or on the stove. Melt 50g (2oz) of the butter in an ovenproof casserole or a saucepan. Add the onion and garlic and fry until the onion is golden, stirring frequently.

2 Add the rice and fry for a further 2 minutes, stirring constantly. Pour in the water and wine and stir in half the salt and half the black pepper. Bring to the boil, cover the pan and either simmer on the stove, or cook in an oven preheated to 350°F, 180°C, Gas Mark 4, for about 20 minutes or until the rice is tender and the liquid has been absorbed.

3 Meanwhile melt the remaining butter in a frying pan and
sauté the mushrooms for 2–3 minutes. Stir in the tomatoes,
oregano and remaining salt and pepper. Allow to simmer for a
further 2–3 minutes. Sprinkle in the diced avocado, stir well,
remove from the heat and keep warm.
4 Arrange the rice in a ring around a large serving plate and
fill the centre with the mushroom and avocado mixture.
Sprinkle with the garnish and serve immediately.

Sultan Reşat pilavi – aubergine and tomato pilav

This is a Turkish classic named after a Sultan who probably
liked it or even helped to create it.

Excellent with roast meat or poultry, particularly kebabs,
but it can also be eaten as a savoury with pickles and yoghurt.

2 large aubergines, peeled and cut into 1cm (½″) cubes
50g (2oz) butter or ghee
1 large onion, roughly chopped
4 large tomatoes, blanched, peeled and chopped
50g (2oz) vermicelli, broken into 2.5cm (1″) pieces
1 teaspoon salt
½ teaspoon black pepper
225g (8oz) long-grain rice, washed thoroughly under cold water and
    drained
900ml (1½ pints) water
A few fresh mint leaves

1 Place the aubergine cubes on a large plate, sprinkle with
salt and set aside for 30 minutes.
2 Meanwhile heat the butter or ghee in a large saucepan, add
the onion and fry until soft. Stir in the tomatoes, vermicelli,
salt and pepper, and fry, stirring frequently for a further
2–3 minutes.
3 Place the aubergine cubes in a colander and rinse
thoroughly. Add them to the saucepan and fry for a few more
minutes, stirring frequently.
4 Stir in the rice, water and mint leaves and bring to the boil.
Lower the heat and simmer for 15–20 minutes or until the rice
is tender and the liquid absorbed.

5 Set aside 'to rest' for 10 minutes, then fluff up with a long-pronged fork and serve.

Paella alcochofas – green artichoke pilav

A wonderful paella from Southern Spain which makes a very tasty accompaniment to roast meats, but it can be eaten as a savoury too.

6 artichokes
1 tablespoon lemon juice
1 tablespoon salt
6 tablespoons olive oil
1 large onion, finely chopped
2 cloves garlic, crushed
3 large tomatoes, blanched, peeled and chopped
1 large red pepper, coarsely chopped
250g (9oz) long-grain rice, washed thoroughly under cold water and
  drained
½ teaspoon saffron
½ teaspoon black pepper

1 Three-quarters fill a large saucepan with water and stir in the lemon juice and salt. Bring to the boil.
2 Meanwhile remove the coarse outer leaves of the artichokes and cut off the stalks. Rub the cut bases with a piece of lemon to prevent discolouring. Taking one artichoke at a time, cut the tips off the leaves, starting with the outer leaves which you cut lowest; then cut the second layer a little higher; the third a little higher still and so on until a cone-shape is left. Rub all the cut edges with lemon. Continue in this way until you have prepared all the artichokes in the same way.
3 Quarter each artichoke and use a small spoon to scrape out and discard the hairy choke. Drop the prepared quarters into the boiling water and simmer for 10–15 minutes or until their bases are tender when pierced with a knife.
4 Heat the oil in a large saucepan, add the onion and garlic and fry for a few minutes until soft. Stir in the tomatoes, red pepper and rice, fry for 2–3 minutes and then remove from the heat.

5 When they are tender strain the artichokes into a colander and retain 600ml (1 pint) of the cooking water. Pour this water onto the rice and stir in the saffron and black pepper.
6 Return the pan to the heat, bring to the boil, lower the heat and simmer for 10 minutes.
7 Remove the cover, stir in the artichokes, cover again and simmer for a further 10 minutes. Remove from the heat, set aside for a few minutes and then serve.

Risi e pisi – rice and pea pilav

This is a North Italian version of a classic Austro-Hungarian dish. It has countless variations, but always with the two basic ingredients of rice and peas. You can add bacon, onions, wine, cheese etc.

It makes a delicious savoury course when served with a mixed salad. The recipe below is sufficient to provide a filling meal for 6–8 people.

1 tablespoon oil
175g (6oz) bacon or ham, chopped
50g (2oz) butter
1 onion, thinly sliced
450g (1lb) shelled peas
350g (12oz) long-grain rice, washed thoroughly under cold water and
  drained
90ml (3fl oz) dry, white wine
720ml (24fl oz) chicken stock or water, boiling
1 teaspoon salt
½ teaspoon black pepper
110g (4oz) grated parmesan cheese (or mixture of parmesan and
  cheddar)

1 Heat the oil in a large saucepan, add the bacon or ham and fry, stirring occasionally, until crisp and golden. Remove with a slotted spoon and drain on kitchen paper.
2 Add 25g (1oz) of the butter to the pan and melt over a moderate heat. Add the onion, and fry, stirring occasionally until soft. Add the peas and rice to the pan, lower the heat and fry for 5 minutes, stirring frequently.

3 Pour in the wine and a third of the stock or water and
simmer until the liquid has been absorbed. Add a further third
of the liquid and cook until absorbed. Add the remaining liquid
and simmer until it has been absorbed and the rice is tender.
4 Stir in the bacon, remaining butter, salt, pepper and cheese.
Cook over a low heat for a further 1–2 minutes and then
transfer to a large dish and serve at once.

Tutum pilav – pumpkin pilav

Pumpkins are badly neglected in the West. However, in the
Middle East, particularly amongst Armenians, Turks and
Kurds, they are highly prized and there are scores of recipes
exploiting the many-sided talents of the simple country
pumpkin!

   This pumpkin pilav is simple and superb. It is quite often
eaten as a main meal with pickles and yoghurt.

250g (9oz) long-grain rice, washed thoroughly under cold water and
   drained
450ml (¾ pint) water
1 teaspoon salt
1 heaped teaspoon dillweed
75g (3oz) sultanas
675g (1½lb) pumpkin, peeled and cut lengthways into 1cm (½″) thick
   slices
75g sugar
110g (4oz) butter, melted

1 Place the rice and water in a saucepan and bring quickly to
the boil. Lower the heat and simmer for 10 minutes. Stir in the
salt, dillweed and sultanas and cook for a further 5 minutes.
Turn immediately into a sieve and run cold water through the
rice.
2 Butter a large, ovenproof baking dish or casserole. Arrange
half the pumpkin slices over the bottom and sprinkle with one
third of the sugar and melted butter.
3 Put the rice into a large bowl, add half the remaining sugar
and butter and mix thoroughly. Spread over the pumpkin
slices.

4 Pour the remaining butter into a frying pan and fry the
remaining pumpkin slices for a few minutes, turning once.
5 Arrange these slices decoratively over the rice and sprinkle
with the remaining sugar and any butter left in the frying pan.
Cover and bake in an oven preheated to 350°F, 180°C, Gas
Mark 4 for 40–45 minutes.
6 Remove from the oven and serve.

Purée de piments au riz – red pepper pilav

I have included two recipes for pepper pilav, one is French and
the other Middle Eastern. Both make tasty pilavs which are
excellent accompaniments for steaks, chops and roast meats.

350g (12oz) long-grain rice, washed thoroughly under cold water and
   drained
720ml (24fl oz) boiling water or stock
1 teaspoon salt
110g (4oz) butter
3 large red peppers, seeded and finely chopped
1 large onion, finely chopped
2 cloves garlic, crushed
½ teaspoon black pepper
½ teaspoon cayenne pepper

1 Place the rice in a large saucepan with the water or stock
and the salt and bring to the boil. Lower the heat, cover and
simmer for 15–20 minutes or until the rice is tender and the
liquid absorbed.
2 Meanwhile melt half the butter in a large pan, add the
peppers and fry for 5 minutes, stirring occasionally. Add the
onion and garlic and fry for a further 5 minutes.
3 Remove the pan from the heat and transfer the pepper
mixture to a blender. Reduce to a purée.
4 Melt the remaining butter in a large pan and stir in the
pepper purée. Season with the black and cayenne peppers.
5 By now the rice should be cooked. Spoon it into the pepper
mixture and stir thoroughly with a wooden spoon. Cover over a
low heat for 2 minutes and then set aside for a few minutes.
Transfer to a large dish and serve.

Bughbeghov pilav – Armenian pepper pilav

110g (4oz) butter
50g (2oz) vermicelli, broken into 2.5cm (1″) pieces
350g (12oz) long-grain rice, washed thoroughly under cold water and
   drained
720ml (24fl oz) boiling water or stock
2 large red peppers, seeded and thinly sliced
2 tablespoons dry white wine
1 teaspoon salt
½ teaspoon allspice
1 teaspoon cumin
½ teaspoon paprika

1 Melt half the butter in a large saucepan, add the vermicelli
and fry for 2–3 minutes or until golden, stirring frequently.
Add the rice and fry for a further 2 minutes, still stirring.
2 Add the water or stock and bring to the boil. Cover the pan,
lower the heat and simmer for 15–20 minutes or until the rice
is tender and the liquid absorbed.
3 Meanwhile melt the remaining butter. Add the peppers and
fry for 5 minutes, stirring occasionally. Stir in all the
remaining ingredients and cook for a further 2–3 minutes.
4 Transfer this mixture to the rice pan and mix thoroughly
with a wooden spoon. Cook for a further 2–3 minutes and then
transfer to a serving dish.

Soongov pilav – pilav with mushrooms

Mushrooms and rice go well together and there are several
such recipes. I have given two. The first is a golden-coloured
pilav with a sharp, lemony flavour from Armenia. The
flavouring comes from sumac which can be bought from
specialist Middle Eastern shops. The second recipe hails from
Greece and has a light, lemon flavour, this time from lemon
rind.

   Both are excellent with kebabs.

50g (2oz) butter
1 large onion, finely chopped
1 large green pepper, thinly sliced

225g (8oz) mushrooms, wiped clean and thickly sliced
2 large tomatoes, blanched, peeled and chopped
2 cloves garlic, crushed
350g (12oz) long-grain rice, washed thoroughly under cold water and
   drained
720ml (24fl oz) boiling water
1 teaspoon salt
½ teaspoon saffron

Garnish:
1 tablespoon sumac

1 Melt the butter in a large saucepan. Add the onion and
green pepper and fry until soft. Add the mushrooms, tomatoes
and garlic and fry for a further 2–3 minutes.
2 Add the rice, water, salt and saffron and stir well. Bring
quickly to the boil, cover the pan, lower the heat and simmer
until the rice is tender and the liquid absorbed.
3 Remove from the heat and set aside 'to rest' for 10 minutes.
Fluff up with a long-pronged fork and transfer to a serving
dish. Sprinkle generously with the sumac and serve.

Pilafi manidari – Greek mushroom pilav

50g (2oz) butter
1 onion, finely chopped
2 cloves garlic, crushed
350g (12oz) long-grain rice, washed thoroughly under cold water and
   drained
350g (12oz) button mushrooms, wiped clean and halved
1 teaspoon salt
½ teaspoon black pepper
1 bay leaf
Thinly pared rind of 1 lemon
720ml (24fl oz) boiling water or stock

Garnish:
1 tablespoon butter
2 tablespoons slivered almonds
1 tablespoon raisins

1 Melt the butter in a large saucepan, add the onion and garlic

and fry until soft. Add the rice and mushrooms and fry for a
further 2–3 minutes, stirring frequently.
2 Stir in all the remaining ingredients and bring to the boil.
Lower the heat, cover the pan and simmer for 15–20 minutes
or until all the liquid has been absorbed.
3 Remove from the heat and set aside 'to rest' for 10 minutes.
4 Meanwhile, to prepare the garnish, melt the butter in a
small pan and fry the almonds and raisins until the almonds
are lightly browned and the raisins puffed up. Remove from
the heat and set aside.
5 When the rice is ready, fluff it up with a long-pronged fork
and transfer to a serving dish. Sprinkle the pilav with the
almonds and raisins and serve immediately.

Chelo sabzamini – rice and potato pilav

A classic Iranian pilav based on the famous 'chelo'.
    An extremely attractive dish with golden brown potato
slices.
    This pilav is often treated as a whole meal and is served with
a bowl of salad, pickles and yoghurt.

350g (12oz) long-grain rice, washed thoroughly under cold water and
    drained
1.5l (2½ pints) water
2 tablespoons salt
½ teaspoon saffron
1 teaspoon sugar
1 teaspoon warm water
75g (3oz) melted butter
2 large potatoes, peeled and cut into slices about 0.5cm (¼″) thick
25g (1oz) butter, cut into small pieces

1 Place the rice in a large bowl, add half the salt and enough
cold water to cover by about 2.5cm (1″). Leave to soak for 2
hours.
2 Bring the water to the boil in a large saucepan with a
close-fitting lid. Drain the rice thoroughly in a sieve, then pour
it slowly into the boiling water and add the remaining salt.
Stir and then boil, uncovered, for 5 minutes.

3 Drain the rice back into the sieve.

4 Mash the saffron and sugar together in a small bowl and add the teaspoon of warm water and the melted butter. Mix well and then pour into the large saucepan. Add the potato slices and turn them to coat with the mixture.

5 Spread the potato slices out evenly over the base of the pan and spoon the rice over the top. Dot the surface with the pieces of butter.

6 Cover the pan, place over a moderate heat and cook for 5 minutes.

7 Remove the lid, cover the pan with a tea towel and replace the lid, making sure that the ends of the towel are kept away from the heat. Reduce the heat as much as possible and leave to steam for 35–40 minutes.

8 To serve, first spoon the rice onto a serving dish and then, using a palette knife, remove the potato slices and arrange them around the rice.

Spanikh-bil-roz – spinach with rice

An Arab speciality which is popular throughout the Middle East.

Use fresh spinach and wash it very thoroughly.

8 tablespoons vegetable oil
1 large onion, finely chopped
450g (1lb) fresh spinach, coarse stems and leaves discarded, washed thoroughly and very coarsely chopped
350g (12oz) long-grain rice, washed thoroughly under cold water and drained
1 teaspoon salt
½ teaspoon black pepper
720ml (24fl oz) boiling water

Garnish:
Lemon wedges

1 Heat the oil in a large saucepan, add the onion and fry until soft.

2 Add the spinach, cover and cook until the spinach is slightly limp.

3 Add the remaining ingredients, but do not stir. Cook over a moderate heat until the water comes to the boil and then lower the heat and simmer until all the liquid has been absorbed.

4 Remove from the heat and allow to 'rest' for 5 minutes.

5 To serve place a large plate on top of the saucepan and then carefully turn the pan upside down and then lift off. The spinach should now form a layer over the rice. Garnish with the lemon wedges and serve.

Tomatoes and rice complement each other brilliantly and there are many variations. I have chosen 3 of the best. The first recipe is the simplest. The second is the famed Turkish 'Domatesli Pilavi', also known throughout the Middle East as 'Istanboli Pilav'. The third is an Indian version and includes ginger and cumin.

Tomato pilav

A typical recipe used throughout the Middle East.

50g (2oz) butter
350g (12oz) long-grain rice, washed thoroughly under cold water and
    drained
450g (1lb) tomatoes, blanched, peeled and chopped
1 teaspoon salt
½ teaspoon black pepper
600ml (1 pint) boiling water or stock

1 Melt the butter in a large saucepan. Add the rice and fry for 2–3 minutes, stirring frequently. Add the remaining ingredients, stir well and bring to the boil. Cover the pan, lower the heat and simmer for 15–20 minutes or until the rice is tender and the liquid absorbed.

2 Remove from the heat and set aside to 'rest' for 10 minutes.

3 Fluff up with a long-pronged fork and serve with roast meats and kebabs.

Domatesli pilavi – Turkish pilav with tomatoes

A delicious pilav.

50g (2oz) butter or ghee
1 onion, finely chopped
2 cloves garlic, finely chopped
4 large tomatoes, blanched, peeled and chopped
1 teaspoon salt
½ teaspoon black pepper
½ teaspoon dried basil
2 tablespoons finely chopped parsley
350g (12oz) long-grain rice, washed thoroughly under cold water and
  drained
600ml (1 pint) boiling water

1 Melt the butter in a large saucepan, add the onion and garlic
and fry until soft. Add the tomatoes, salt, pepper, basil, parsley
and rice and fry for a further 2–3 minutes, stirring frequently.
2 Pour in the water and bring quickly to the boil. Cover the
pan, lower the heat and simmer for 15–20 minutes or until the
rice is tender and the liquid has been absorbed.
3 Set aside to 'rest' for 10 minutes and then fluff up with a
long-pronged fork and serve.

Tamatar pilao – Indian tomato pilav

A simple, but tasty pilav from the Indian sub-continent. It
makes an ideal accompaniment to roast and grilled dishes.

50g (2oz) butter or ghee
1 large onion, finely chopped
2 cloves garlic, crushed
2.5cm (1″) piece fresh ginger, peeled and finely chopped
1 large red pepper, seeded and thinly sliced
350g (12oz) long-grain rice, washed thoroughly under cold water and
  drained
450g (1lb) tomatoes, blanched, peeled and chopped
1 teaspoon salt
1 teaspoon cumin
¼ teaspoon black pepper
600ml (1 pint) boiling water

Garnish:
3–4 tablespoons thinly sliced spring onions

1 Melt the butter or ghee in a large saucepan. Add the onion, garlic and ginger and fry, stirring frequently, until the onion is soft. Add the red pepper and fry for a further 3 minutes. Stir in the rice.
2 Add all the remaining ingredients and mix well. Bring quickly to the boil and then cover the pan, reduce the heat to very low and simmer for 15–20 minutes or until the rice is tender and the liquid absorbed.
3 Remove the pan from the heat and spoon the pilav into a large dish. Sprinkle with the spring onions and serve.

Rizi dhaktilidhi – Greek vegetable pilav

A very attractive Greek vegetable pilav that is moulded into a ring and garnished with olives. Delicately flavoured with herbs it goes well with pork and lamb and is equally delicious served cold as a salad.

1.5l (2½ pints) water
1 teaspoon salt
1 teaspoon lemon juice
350g (12oz) long-grain rice, washed thoroughly under cold water and
  drained
3 tomatoes, finely chopped
3 tablespoons chopped chives
3 tablespoons chopped parsley
15 green olives, stoned and chopped
1 level teaspoon dried basil
1 level teaspoon dried marjoram
1 red pepper, seeded and finely chopped
7–8 tablespoons olive oil
3 tablespoons vinegar
1½ teaspoons salt
½ teaspoon black pepper

Garnish:
Black olives

1 Place the water in a large saucepan with the salt and lemon juice and bring to the boil. Add the rice and simmer for 12–15 minutes or until the rice is only just tender. Drain the rice into a colander and cover with a clean cloth.

2 Put the tomatoes, chives, parsley, green olives, basil, marjoram and red pepper into a large bowl and mix well. Add the rice and stir until all the ingredients are well distributed.

3 Mix the oil, vinegar, salt and pepper together in a small bowl and then add enough of it to the rice mixture to moisten and season it thoroughly.

4 Press the rice into a 1.8l (3 pint) ring mould and cover with buttered foil.

5 Pour boiling water into a large roasting tin to a depth of about 1cm (½″) and place the mould in it. Cook over a gentle heat for 15–20 minutes.

6 Place a serving plate over the mould and then invert it. Shake it gently and then lift off the mould. Garnish with the black olives and serve.

Puntsin – African vegetable pilav

This recipe from West Africa is particularly popular in Nigeria. You can vary the vegetables depending on availability and personal taste.

250g (9oz) long-grain rice, washed thoroughly under cold water and
    drained
600ml (1 pint) boiling water or stock
1 teaspoon salt
50g (2oz) butter or ghee
1 large onion, finely chopped
2 large tomatoes, blanched, peeled and chopped
1 green pepper, seeded and chopped
2 sticks celery, trimmed and chopped
175g (6oz) broccoli, broken into small sprigs
175g (6oz) mushrooms, wiped clean and chopped
2 tablespoons finely chopped parsley
50g (2oz) salted peanuts
½ teaspoon cayenne pepper
½ teaspoon black pepper

1 Put the rice into a large saucepan, add the water or stock and the salt and bring to the boil. Boil vigorously for 1 minute, cover the pan, lower the heat and simmer for 15–20 minutes or until all the liquid has been absorbed.
2 Remove from the heat and leave 'to rest'.
3 Meanwhile in another large pan melt the butter or ghee, add the onion and fry until soft. Add all the remaining vegetables and fry for about 5 minutes, stirring frequently, until the vegetables are just tender.
4 Add the parsley, peanuts, cayenne and black pepper and the cooked rice and mix gently with a wooden spoon. Cook over a low heat for a further 2–3 minutes, stirring occasionally.
5 Remove from the heat, spoon into a large dish and serve immediately.

Moghlai pilau – Mogul-style rice pilau

'Tastefully did I cook the rice,
And come to you at midnight.
Alas! nowhere did I find you, my love!
For the rest of my life I will weep for you.'
        'The Unwritten Song' VII

A magnificent pilav worthy of the Mogul emperors. A meal in itself.

600ml (1 pint) water
1 teaspoon salt
350g (12oz) long-grain rice, washed thoroughly under cold water and
  drained
2 tablespoons butter
2 large carrots, peeled and thinly sliced
1 large onion, sliced
110g (4oz) peas
110g (4oz) french beans, topped and tailed and then cut into 5cm (2″)
  pieces
2 courgettes, thinly sliced
110g (4oz) broad beans, shelled and with transparent skins removed
110g (4oz) ghee or butter
1 teaspoon black cumin seeds

5cm (2″) cinnamon stick
4–5 green cardamoms
2 cloves garlic, crushed
2 green chillis, finely chopped
1 tablespoon poppy seeds
50g (2oz) cashew nuts
2 teaspoons coriander seeds
2.5cm (1″) fresh ginger, finely chopped OR 1 teaspoon ground ginger
300ml (½ pint) yoghurt

1 Place the water and salt in a saucepan and bring to the boil.
Add the rice, cover the pan, lower the heat and simmer until
the water has been absorbed. Set aside.
2 Melt the 2 tablespoons of the butter in a large pan. Add all
the vegetables and fry, stirring frequently with a wooden
spoon, for about 5 minutes. Remove the pan from the heat and
reserve.
3 Melt half the ghee or butter in a large pan, add the cumin
seeds and fry for 1 minute. Add the cinnamon stick,
cardamoms and the cooked rice and fry for 2–3 minutes,
stirring frequently until well mixed.
4 With a mortar and pestle, or in a blender, grind together the
garlic, chillis, poppy seeds, cashew nuts, coriander seeds and
ginger. Add 2–3 tablespoons of water if necessary to form a
thick paste.
5 In a small pan melt the remaining ghee or butter. Add the
garlic mixture and fry for 2 minutes. Remove from the heat
and stir in the yoghurt.
6 Grease a large ovenproof casserole and spread half the rice
mixture over the base. Spoon the yoghurt mixture evenly over
it and then top with the vegetables. Spread the remaining rice
over the top. Cover the pan and cook in an oven preheated to
400°F, 200°C, Gas Mark 6 for 20 minutes. Remove from the
oven and serve immediately.

Rice with Fruit and Nuts

'When he called his lupins sweeter than almonds, he was answered, "a deceit only fit for children"' – *Ancient Egyptian saying*

With rice anything goes.

Particularly successful are nuts. Almonds, pistachios, walnuts and hazelnuts appear throughout the Middle Eastern lands. Further east occur cashew nuts, chestnuts, ginkgo nuts and, of course, coconuts. Peanuts are much used in Africa and parts of America.

As for fruits – both fresh and dried varieties are used. The most popular ones are dates, raisins, apricots, prunes, oranges, lemons, pineapples, quinces and bananas.

The simple white of the rice grain can thus be transformed to a multi-coloured, magical experience.

Noushov pilav – pilav with almonds

This is a very popular pilav from Turkey and Armenia. The raisins give the pilav a slightly sweetish tinge while the golden almonds make a strong visual and textural contrast.

The Lebanese prefer to use pine kernels instead of almonds. I, personally, like a combination of the two. You can also use pistachios, hazelnuts or walnuts.

50g (2oz) butter or ghee
350g (12oz) long-grain rice, washed under cold water and drained
1 teaspoon salt
720ml (24fl oz) boiling water
50g (2oz) raisins
25g (1oz) butter
75g (3oz) blanched almonds
Pinch salt

1 Melt the 50g (2oz) butter or ghee in a large pan. Add the rice and fry for 2–3 minutes, stirring frequently. Stir in the salt, water and raisins and boil vigorously for 1 minute. Lower the heat, cover the pan and simmer for 15–20 minutes or until all

the liquid has been absorbed. Turn off the heat and set aside to 'rest'.

2 Now melt the 25g (1oz) butter in a small pan, add the almonds and fry, stirring frequently, until golden. Remove the almonds with a slotted spoon and drain on kitchen paper. Sprinkle with a pinch of salt.

3 Gently fluff up the pilav with a long-pronged fork and transfer to a large dish. Sprinkle with the almonds and serve.

Shirini pollo – sweet nut and sultana pilav

A classic Iranian pilav which is excellent with kebabs and other meat dishes. Small pieces of cooked chicken are often included in the fruit and nut mixture.

2 oranges
50g (2oz) butter or ghee
150ml (¼ pint) water
75g (3oz) sugar
pinch saffron dissolved in 1 tablespoon warm water
2 carrots, peeled and cut into thin sticks
75g (3oz) shelled pistachio nuts
50g (2oz) slivered almonds
50g (2oz) sultanas
5cm (2″) cinnamon stick
1 tablespoon lemon juice
350g (12oz) long-grain rice, washed thoroughly under cold water and
    drained
1 tablespoon salt

1 Cut the peel from the oranges in thin strips. Discard any white pith and then cut the peel into thin strips. Place them in a pan and cover with lightly salted, cold water. Bring to the boil, lower the heat and cook until soft.

2 Remove from the heat, drain and rinse with cold water. Dry with kitchen paper.

3 In a small saucepan melt the butter over a moderate heat. Add the water, sugar and dissolved saffron and heat, stirring constantly until the sugar has dissolved. Add the orange peel, sliced carrots, pistachios, almonds, sultanas, cinnamon stick

and lemon juice. Squeeze the juice out of the two oranges and stir into the pan. Simmer over a low heat until the mixture has thickened and much of the water has evaporated. Remove from the heat and reserve.

4 Half fill a large saucepan with water and bring to the boil. Add the rice in a steady stream so as not to disturb the boiling and stir in the salt. Boil for 8 minutes and then drain immediately and rinse with cold water. Set aside to drain well.

5 Generously grease a large casserole. Spread half the rice over the base. Discard the cinnamon stick and then arrange the nut and sultana mixture over the rice. Layer the remaining rice over the top. Cover the casserole with a tight-fitting lid and cook in an oven preheated to 350°F, 180°C, Gas Mark 4 for 30 minutes. Remove from the oven and serve.

Coconut rice

There are several versions of this simple idea of combining rice and coconut. In South-East Asia coconut milk (page 00) is mixed with rice and salt and forms the basis of many Indonesian, Burmese, Thai and Filippino meals. I have included two recipes below, one from Burma and one from the West Indies.

Ohn htamin – Burmese coconut rice

350g (12oz) long-grain rice, washed under cold water and drained
1l (1¾ pints) coconut milk
2 teaspoons salt

1 Place the rice, coconut milk and salt in a large saucepan and bring to the boil. Boil for 2 minutes and then lower the heat and stir the mixture vigorously. Cover the pan and simmer for 25 minutes.

2 Remove the lid and check that all the coconut milk has been absorbed. If not, stir lightly with a wooden spoon around the edges of the pan. Cover and continue to simmer for a further 5–10 minutes.

3 Serve with curries, stews and roasts.

West Indian coconut rice

Although this recipe is from the Caribbean its origins are
undoubtedly Indian.

Fresh coconuts can be found all the year round in Indian
shops.

Serve with all types of curry dishes, stews and casseroles.

50g (2oz) butter or ghee
1 onion, finely chopped
350g (12oz) long-grain rice, washed thoroughly under cold water and
  drained
300ml (½ pint) water
450ml (¾ pint) coconut milk
1½ teaspoons salt

Garnish:
½ fresh coconut OR 75g (3oz) flaked or desiccated coconut

1 Melt the butter or ghee in a large pan. Add the onion and fry
until soft, stirring frequently. Add the rice and fry for a further
2–3 minutes, still stirring frequently.
2 Add the water, coconut milk and salt and stir well. Bring to
the boil and allow to bubble vigorously for 1 minute. Lower the
heat, cover the pan and simmer for 20 minutes or until all the
liquid has been absorbed.
3 Meanwhile, if using fresh coconut, remove its brown, outer
skin with a sharp knife. Cut the flesh into thin flakes. Line a
baking sheet with foil and spread the flakes out on it. If using
flaked or desiccated coconut spread it out in the same way.
Place the tray under a medium-hot grill and cook until golden.
Stir frequently and take care not to burn.
4 When the rice is cooked pile it into a serving dish and top
with the toasted coconut. Serve immediately.

Variation: You can include in the rice 2 tablespoons raisins
soaked in a little rum for 1 hour and 2 tablespoons blanched
almonds. Garnish with fresh tarragon leaves.

Pineapple and cashew nut pilav

A West Indian pilav of East Indian origin!

Marvellous colours, textures and discordant ingredients which combine to create a most original pilav which can be eaten as a savoury or, preferably, as an accompaniment to pork and fowl dishes.

75g (3oz) butter
350g (12oz) fresh pineapple, cut into chunks. You can use tinned pineapple chunks, but if you do, choose those in a natural juice
50g (2oz) raisins
10 spring onions, trimmed and chopped
75g (3oz) cashew nuts
1 tablespoon coriander seeds, coarsely crushed OR 1 teaspoon ground coriander
½ teaspoon cayenne pepper
350g (12oz) long-grain rice, washed thoroughly under cold water and drained
1 teaspoon salt
600ml (1 pint) boiling water or chicken stock

1 Melt half the butter in a saucepan, add the pineapple chunks and raisins and fry, turning frequently, for 2–3 minutes or until the pineapple is lightly coloured. Remove the pan from the heat and set aside.
2 Melt the remaining butter in a large pan, add the spring onions and fry, stirring occasionally, until they are golden. Add the cashew nuts, coriander and cayenne pepper and fry, stirring frequently, for a further 2–3 minutes.
3 Add the rice and salt and fry, stirring constantly for another 3–4 minutes.
4 Stir in the pineapple and raisin mixture and pour in the boiling water or stock. When boiling vigorously, lower the heat, cover the pan and simmer for about 20 minutes or until all the liquid has been absorbed.
5 Leave to 'rest' for 10 minutes and then serve.

Roz-bil-tamar – almond and date pilav

'If you give my son a date, my stomach will taste its sweetness.' – *Arab proverb*

A classic from Arabia, perhaps one of the few genuine Bedouin dishes that have survived to our day and, like all Bedouin dishes it is simple and wholesome.

50g (2oz) butter
350g (12oz) long-grain rice, washed thoroughly under cold water and
  drained
1 teaspoon salt
720ml (24fl oz) boiling water

Garnish:
50g (2oz) butter
50g (2oz) blanched almonds
75g (3oz) stoned dates, chopped
50g (2oz) raisins or sultanas
1 teaspoon rosewater

1 Melt the butter in a large saucepan, add the rice and fry for 2–3 minutes, stirring frequently. Add the salt and boiling water. Boil vigorously for 1 minute and then cover, lower the heat and simmer for 15–20 minutes or until all the liquid has been absorbed. Turn off the heat and leave 'to rest' for 10 minutes.
2 Meanwhile melt the butter for the garnish in a large frying pan. Add the almonds and fry, stirring frequently, until they begin to turn a light golden colour. Add the dried fruits and fry for a few more minutes, stirring frequently. Remove from the heat and stir in the rosewater.
3 To serve, fluff up the rice with a long-pronged fork and pile it into a large dish. Spoon the date and almond mixture over the top and serve at once.

Sergevilov pilav – quince and walnut pilav

Quinces not only make delicious jams, but are much used in many aspects of Middle Eastern cooking. They are particularly good with pork and lamb. This Armenian pilav is delightful. Serve it with any kind of pork or lamb stew or roast.

You can substitute cooking apples for the quinces, since the latter only appear in late autumn.

350g (12oz) long-grain rice, washed thoroughly under cold water and drained
½ teaspoon salt
450ml (¾ pint) water
150ml (¼ pint) dry white wine
2 tablespoons unsalted butter or ghee
2 medium quinces OR cooking apples, peeled, cored and cut into 2.5cm (1″) chunks
2 tablespoons sugar
¼ teaspoon nutmeg
¼ teaspoon cinnamon
50g (2oz) chopped walnuts

1 Place the rice, salt, water and wine in a large saucepan and bring to the boil. Stir vigorously and then cover the pan, lower the heat and simmer for 15–20 minutes or until the liquid has been absorbed.
2 Meanwhile melt the butter in a frying pan and add the quinces, sugar, nutmeg, cinnamon and walnuts. Cook over a moderate heat, turning gently, until the quince pieces are just tender. Do not overcook or the fruit will turn to pulp.
3 Fold this mixture gently into the cooked rice and steam over a low heat for a further 3–5 minutes. Turn off the heat and leave 'to rest' for 10 minutes before serving.

Riz au citron – lemon pilav

'He thinks himself a lemon in a nauseated town.' – *Arab saying*

A French speciality that goes extremely well with fish and poultry dishes.

600ml (1 pint) water
350g (12oz) long-grain rice, washed thoroughly under cold water and drained
1½ teaspoons salt

4 eggs
175g (6oz) parmesan OR cheddar cheese, or a mixture of the two,
 grated
Rind of 2 medium lemons, grated
2 tablespoons lemon juice
25g (1oz) butter

1 Bring the water to the boil in a large saucepan. Stir in the
rice and salt and boil for 2 minutes. Lower the heat, cover the
pan and simmer for 15–20 minutes or until all the liquid has
been absorbed. Turn off the heat and leave 'to rest' for a few
minutes.
2 Beat the eggs thoroughly in a bowl. Add the cheese, lemon
rind and lemon juice and mix together.
3 Melt the butter in a large pan and add the rice. Pour the egg
and cheese mixture over the rice and mix thoroughly. Cook
over a moderate heat, stirring constantly, until the cheese
melts. Turn into a large dish and serve immediately.

Naranji pilau – orange pilav

A beautiful dish from Kashmir in Northern India.
 Serve it with any kind of curry or roast. It goes particularly
well with pork and chicken dishes.

50g (2oz) butter or ghee
2 medium onions, thinly sliced
75g (3oz) cashew nuts
25g (1oz) raisins
Peel of ½ orange, white pith discarded, cut into thin (match-stick size)
 strips
3 cardamom pods
4 cloves
5cm (2″) cinnamon stick
Juice 2 large oranges
350g (12oz) long-grain rice, washed thoroughly under cold water and
 drained
1 teaspoon salt

1 Melt the butter or ghee in a large pan, add the onion and fry
until soft, stirring regularly. Add the cashew nuts, raisins and

orange rind and fry for 2–3 minutes, stirring frequently.

2 Add the remaining ingredients and mix well.

3 Measure the orange juice and make up to 720ml (24fl oz) with boiling water. Stir this into the rice mixture and bring to the boil. Lower the heat, cover the pan and simmer for about 20 minutes or until all the liquid has been absorbed. Set aside 'to rest' for 10 minutes.

4 Fluff the pilav up gently with a long-pronged fork, turn into a large dish and serve.

Japanese fruit and nut gohans

'As the ears of rice
On the autumn fields
Bend in one direction,
So with one mind would I bend you,
Painfully though the gossip be.' – *Ten Thousand Leaves*

'Gohan' in Japanese means 'honourable food'. It is also the name for rice. Plain, boiled rice may still be the staple food of the land, but there are many variations which make use of vegetables and meat cuts. There are also some fascinating dishes that are prepared with cherry blossom (Sakura Gohan), which has a very distinctive fragrance. The cherry blossoms are preserved in salt and are sold in bottles. Another unusual (to most Westerners) rice dish is new tea rice (Shincha Gohan) where the rice is prepared with fresh tea leaves. Other rice dishes use flower petals, ginkgo nuts, chestnuts etc. The preparation method is simple and you can experiment with any fruit or nut of your liking. Below is a recipe for chestnut rice which is traditionally eaten in the autumn.

Kuri gohan – chestnut rice

30 fresh chestnuts OR 450g (1lb) tinned chestnuts, drained
350g (12oz) short-grain rice, washed thoroughly under cold water and
   drained
1½ teaspoons salt
600ml (1 pint) water
4 tablespoons saké

1 If using fresh chestnuts, slit the skin of each around the
middle and place in a saucepan. Cover with water and bring to
the boil. Lower the heat and simmer for 5 minutes. Remove
and drain. Peel and skin each chestnut and place in a bowl.
Cover with cold water and leave to soak for 30 minutes. Drain.
2 Place all the ingredients in a large saucepan and bring to
the boil. Lower the heat, cover the pan and simmer until all the
liquid has been absorbed.
3 Remove the pan from the heat and leave 'to rest' for 5–10
minutes before serving.

Ginnan gohan – ginkgo nut rice

Ginkgo nuts are the fruit of *Salisburia sm*, from the family of
Gynkgoaceae.
   It is better known as the Maidenhead Tree.
   Fresh nuts are difficult to find in Britain, but canned ones
can be found in Chinese (pai kuo) and Japanese shops.
   The nut is white and shaped like a small marble. It is never
eaten raw.

30–40 fresh or tinned ginkgo nuts
350g (12oz) short-grain rice, washed thoroughly under cold water and
   drained
600ml (1 pint) water
1½ teaspoons salt
2 tablespoons soy sauce
3 tablespoons saké

1 If using fresh ginkgo nuts place them in a saucepan and
cover with water. Bring to the boil and then lower the heat and
simmer. Press and stir the nuts with the back of a slotted spoon
to loosen the skins. After 5 minutes, drain and remove the
skins by rubbing the nuts in a clean tea towel.
2 Place all the ingredients in a large saucepan and cook as in
the recipe Kuri gohan above. Leave to 'rest' for 5–10 minutes.
3 Serve hot as a pilav or allow to cool to room temperature and
serve as 'rice balls' (see page 26).

Harsaniki pilav – wedding pilav

This exotic pilav comes from Yerevan, in Armenia and it
incorporates dried apricots, prunes, raisins, almonds etc. It is
appropriate therefore to call this 'Wedding Pilav' for only at
such happy occasions were people in the past able to treat
themselves to such luxury.

50g (2oz) butter
1 onion, thinly sliced
2 sticks celery, thinly sliced
350g (12oz) long-grain rice, washed thoroughly under cold water and
  drained
1 teaspoon salt
½ teaspoon ground ginger
720ml (24fl oz) boiling water

Sauce:
50g (2oz) butter
50g (2oz) dried apricots, soaked overnight
50g (2oz) dried prunes, stoned and soaked overnight
50g (2oz) raisins or sultanas
50g (2oz) blanched almonds, chopped
2 tablespoons honey
1 tablespoon hot water

1 Melt the butter in a large saucepan. Add the onion and
celery and fry for about 5 minutes or until soft. Add the rice,
salt and ginger and fry for a further 2–3 minutes. Pour in the
boiling water and stir well. Boil vigorously for 1 minute and
then lower the heat, cover the pan and simmer for 15–20
minutes or until all the liquid has been absorbed. Set aside 'to
rest' for about 10 minutes.
2 Meanwhile prepare the sauce by draining the apricots and
prunes and halving them. Melt the butter in a saucepan, add
all the fruits and nuts and fry, stirring frequently until the
nuts are lightly browned. Mix the honey and water together
and add to the pan. Lower the heat and cook for about 10
minutes, stirring frequently, until the mixture has thickened.
3 To serve, pile the pilav onto a serving dish and pour the
sauce over the top.

Rice with Meat

Rice and meat go well together. The most successful
combination is undoubtedly that of rice and lamb – hence the
numerous dishes that abound in the cuisines of Asia, Africa
and Southern Europe. However, lamb can often be substituted
by beef, and in South-East Asia pork dominates all the
cuisines.

Missov pilav – lamb pilav

This recipe from the Caucasus is simple daily fare, which is
served with yoghurt, a bowl of fresh salad and home-made
pickles.

50g (2oz) butter
1kg (2lb) shoulder or leg of lamb, trimmed of fat, cut into 2.5cm (1″)
  chunks
350g (12oz) long-grain rice, washed thoroughly under cold water and
  drained
1 tablespoon tomato purée
1 teaspoon salt
½ teaspoon black pepper
1 teaspoon thyme or dillweed
600ml (1 pint) boiling water or meat stock

1 Melt the butter in a large pan, add the meat and fry for
5 minutes, stirring frequently. Lower the heat, cover the pan
and cook the meat for about 45 minutes, stirring occasionally
to prevent sticking.
2 Stir in the rice and fry for 2–3 minutes. Add the tomato
purée, salt, black pepper and thyme or dillweed and fry for
another 2–3 minutes, stirring constantly.
3 Pour in the boiling water or stock and boil vigorously for
1 minute. Lower the heat, cover the pan and simmer for about
20 minutes or until the liquid has evaporated. Leave 'to rest'
for a few minutes and then pile into a large dish and serve.

The recipe above is a basic one. You can vary the ingredients by adding other spices and herbs, vegetables and fruits to the basic meat and rice. Below are four suggested variations.

Ajem pilavi – Iranian lamb pilav

This is a Turkish dish, but as the name suggests, it is of Iranian origin. Follow the recipe above but:
1) fry 1 chopped onion with the meat and
2) add 1 teaspoon cinnamon, 2–3 chopped, blanched and peeled tomatoes and 2 tablespoons chopped almonds or pistachios when the rice is added to the meat.

Uzbek plov – Central Asian meat pilav

Follow the recipe 'Missov pilav' above but:
1) fry 2 chopped onions and 1 clove crushed garlic in the butter before adding the meat and
2) peel and finely chop 450g (1lb) carrots and add to the pan, together with 1 tablespoon chopped fresh marjoram OR 1½ teaspoons dried marjoram, when the rice is added.

Baghali pollo – lamb pilav with broad beans

Dill gives this Iranian dish a delicious aroma.

50g (2oz) butter
1 large onion, thinly sliced
1kg (2lb) shoulder or leg lamb, trimmed of fat, cut into 2.5cm (1″)
  chunks
300ml (½ pint) water
1 teaspoon salt
½ teaspoon black pepper
½ teaspoon cinnamon
350g (12oz) long-grain rice, washed thoroughly under cold water and
  drained
1 tablespoon salt
50g (2oz) butter, melted
450g (1lb) broad beans, outer transparent skins removed
3–4 tablespoons chopped fresh dill or 2 teaspoons dried dillweed

1 Melt 50g (2oz) butter in a large pan, add the onion and fry
until soft. Stir in the meat and fry for 5 minutes, turning
occasionally with a wooden spoon. Add the water, salt, pepper
and cinnamon and bring to the boil. Lower the heat, cover the
pan and simmer for 45 minutes, or until the meat is tender.
2 Meanwhile half fill a large pan with water, add the
tablespoon of salt and bring to the boil. Add the rice and boil
for just 5 minutes. Remove from the heat, drain into a colander
and rinse with cold water.
3 Grease a large, ovenproof casserole with some of the melted
butter. Mix the rice, broad beans and dill together in a bowl
and spread half of this mixture over the base of the casserole.
Transfer the meat and onion mixture to the rice with a slotted
spoon and spread out evenly. Top with the remaining beans
and rice. Pour any remaining meat liquid and the rest of the
melted butter over the rice. Cover the pan and cook in an oven
preheated to 350°F, 180°C, Gas Mark 4 for 30 minutes. Remove
from the oven and serve.

Other vegetables, and pulses, can be cooked in this same way
with meat and rice e.g. peas, green beans, tomatoes, split peas,
lentils, chickpeas etc. A particularly nice dish is the one below
from Kurdistan, where long, bulbous pumpkins scatter the
countryside.
    Pumpkins are sold throughout most of the year in Indian
and Chinese shops, but can only be found in autumn in most
greengrocers. However, if not available it is perfectly
acceptable to use other gourds or large courgettes.
    Serve with a bowl of mixed salad and pickles.

Kadu pilavi – pumpkin with meatballs and rice

1kg (2lb) minced lamb
1 large onion, very finely chopped
1 teaspoon salt
½ teaspoon black pepper
½ teaspoon cinnamon
¼ teaspoon nutmeg
½ teaspoon dried mint

50g (2oz) butter
225g (8oz) long-grain rice, washed thoroughly under cold water and
  drained
1 teaspoon salt
675g (1½lb) small pumpkin, peeled and cut into 2.5cm (1″) cubes
2–3 tablespoons brown sugar
75g (3oz) butter, melted

1 Place the lamb, onion, salt, black pepper, cinnamon, nutmeg
and dried mint in a large bowl. Keeping your hand damp with
warm water knead the mixture until well blended and smooth.
Shape the mixture into walnut-sized balls.
2 Melt the 50g (2oz) of butter in a large frying pan, add the
meatballs, a few at a time, and cook for 8–10 minutes, turning
occasionally until evenly browned. Remove with a slotted
spoon and set aside.
3 Half fill a large saucepan with water and bring to the boil.
Add the rice and salt and simmer for 5 minutes. Remove from
the heat, drain and rinse with cold water.
3 Lightly grease a large, ovenproof casserole. Spread half the
rice evenly over the base. Pour half the melted butter over it
and then arrange the meatballs on the rice. Top with the
remaining rice.
4 Arrange the pumpkin pieces on top of the rice, sprinkle with
the sugar and then dribble with the remaining butter. Cover
the casserole and cook in an oven preheated to 375°F, 190°C,
Gas Mark 5 for 20–30 minutes or until the rice and pumpkin
are tender. Remove from the oven and serve.

Kalma pollo – meatballs in rice

You can use beef instead of lamb for this recipe.

1kg (2lb) minced lamb
1 large onion, very finely chopped
1½ teaspoons salt
½ teaspoon black pepper
6 tablespoons butter
1 large cabbage, coarse leaves and core discarded, finely shredded
300ml (½ pint) stock or water

½ teaspoon saffron dissolved in 2 tablespoons warm water
Juice 1 small lemon
1 tablespoon salt
350g (12oz) long-grain rice, washed thoroughly under cold water and
  drained

1 Place the meat, onion, salt and pepper in a large bowl and
knead with damp hands until smooth. Shape into walnut-sized
balls.
2 Melt 2 tablespoons of the butter in a large, heavy-based pan.
Add the meatballs and fry until they are all evenly browned.
Add the shredded cabbage and fry for 2–3 minutes, turning
carefully. Stir in the stock, dissolved saffron and lemon juice
and bring to the boil. Lower the heat and simmer, uncovered,
for 30–40 minutes. Turn occasionally and add a little more
water if necessary.
3 Meanwhile half fill a large saucepan with water and bring to
the boil. Add the salt and rice and boil for 5 minutes. Drain,
rinse under cold water and drain again.
4 Melt the remaining butter in a large pan. Mix 60ml (2fl oz)
of the meat and cabbage stock with a quarter of the rice and
spread over the base of the pan. Spread another quarter of the
rice over it and then cover with the meat and cabbage mixture.
Top evenly with the remaining rice.
5 Wrap the lid with a tea towel and cover the rice tightly.
Steam over a medium-low heat for 30 minutes or until the rice
is tender.
6 The crust (ta-dig) at the bottom of the pan can be cut into
wedges and served separately.

Keema mattar pilau – minced meat and peas with rice

'He used to eat peas, but bad luck foiled him' – *Arab expression*

A simple, cheap and wholesome meal. Serve with yoghurt and
pickles or salad.

50g (2oz) ghee or butter
1 large onion, finely chopped
2 cloves garlic, crushed

1 teaspoon cumin seeds, crushed
1 teaspoon finely chopped fresh ginger
5 cloves
350g (12oz) minced lamb
225g (8oz) peas
1½ teaspoons salt
½ teaspoon black pepper
350g (12oz) long-grain rice, washed thoroughly under cold water and
   drained
720ml (24fl oz) water
1 teaspoon garam masala

1 Melt the ghee in a large saucepan, add the onion and fry
until soft. Stir in the garlic, cumin, ginger and cloves and fry
for 2–3 minutes. Add the minced meat and fry for 8–10
minutes, stirring frequently and breaking up the lumps with a
wooden spoon.
2 Add the peas, salt, black pepper and a little water and cook
over a moderate heat for 15–20 minutes until the meat is
cooked and the water has evaporated.
3 Stir in the rice and water and bring to the boil. Lower the
heat, cover and simmer for 15 minutes. Remove the lid, stir in
the garam masala and cook for a further 5–10 minutes or until
the rice is tender and the water has evaporated.

Biryani

There is a charming legend about a Sassanian king, Khosrow
Parviz, whose daughter Poorandokht was very fond of yoghurt
and yoghurt-based dishes, so much so that all dishes cooked
with yoghurt came to be called 'Poorani' and, eventually
'Borani'. The Indian Biryani-named dishes were developed
much later – during the heyday of the Moghul Emperors.
Biryanis are rice dishes cooked in one pot with meat,
vegetables, fish, etc., but each ingredient is kept in a separate
layer, while Borani dishes are stews which do not include rice,
but most of which contain yoghurt. Who influenced whom?
   Biryani is the royal dish amongst the numerously rich rice
dishes of the Indian subcontinent. It is served on special

occasions and housewives have, over the ages put all their artistry into it.

The first recipe, a masterpiece, does use yoghurt. Although lamb is specified you can use beef or chicken instead.

Moghlai biryani – Moghul-style biryani

1 medium onion, finely chopped
1 teaspoon salt
2 cloves garlic, crushed
1 teaspoon chilli pepper
5 tablespoons ground almonds
2 teaspoons poppy seeds
1½ teaspoons ground cumin
½ teaspoon ground cardamom
1kg (2lb) lamb or beef, cut into 5cm (2″) chunks OR small chops
75g (3oz) ghee or butter
1 onion, thinly sliced
150ml (¼ pint) yoghurt
90ml (3fl oz) water
350g (12oz) long-grain rice, washed thoroughly under cold water and
    drained
5cm (2″) cinnamon stick
3–4 whole cloves
5–6 peppercorns
1½ teaspoons salt
¼ teaspoon saffron dissolved in 2 tablespoons warm water

Garnish:
25g (1oz) ghee or butter
1 tablespoon blanched almonds
1 tablespoon pistachio nuts, halved
3 tablespoons sultanas

1 Place the onion, salt, garlic, chilli pepper, almonds, poppy seeds, cumin, and cardamom in a large bowl and mix well. Add the meat and knead the spices into it. Cover and set aside.
2 Melt half the ghee or butter in a saucepan, add the sliced onion and fry until soft. Add the meat and spice mixture and fry over a low heat for 8–10 minutes, stirring frequently. Stir

in the yoghurt and water and cover the pan. Simmer for about
45 minutes or until tender.
3 Meanwhile half fill a large saucepan with water and bring to
the boil. Add the rice and boil for 5 minutes. Drain the rice,
rinse with cold water and drain again.
4 Melt the remaining ghee or butter in a pan, add the
cinnamon stick, cloves, peppercorns and drained rice and fry
for 2–3 minutes, stirring constantly. Add the salt and
dissolved saffron and stir until the rice is evenly coloured.
5 Lightly grease a large, ovenproof casserole. Spread half the
rice over the base and spoon the cooked meat and any
remaining liquid over it. Cover evenly with the remaining rice.
Fit the lid on tightly and place in an oven preheated to 350°F,
180°C, Gas Mark 4. Cook for 30 minutes or until the rice is
tender.
6 Just before serving prepare the garnish by heating the ghee
or butter in a small pan and frying the nuts and sultanas until
golden. Arrange the biryani on a large plate and scatter with
the garnish.

Khima biryani – minced meat biryani

You can use minced lamb, beef, chicken or even pork –
although I am aware that the latter is sacrilege to many people
from the Indian sub-continent.
 This is a simple and cheap dish which is full of flavour.

1kg (2lb) minced meat
2 cloves garlic, crushed
1 teaspoon salt
1 teaspoon ground coriander
2 green chillis, very finely chopped
½ teaspoon cumin
½ teaspoon ground ginger
2 tablespoons tomato purée
150ml (¼ pint) yoghurt
50g (2oz) ghee or butter
1 large onion, chopped
1 large or 2 medium potatoes, peeled and thinly sliced

350g (12oz) long-grain rice, washed thoroughly under cold water and
  drained
1 tablespoon salt
225g (8oz) of any of the following: split lentils, whole lentils, chickpeas
  or fresh peas, cooked until just tender
50g butter or ghee, cut into small pieces

1 Place the minced meat in a saucepan with the garlic, salt,
coriander, chillis, cumin, ginger and tomato purée. Fry over a
medium heat for 20–30 minutes, stirring frequently and
breaking up lumps with a wooden spoon. Stir in the yoghurt
thoroughly, remove the pan from the heat and set aside.
2 Meanwhile melt the ghee or butter in a frying pan, add the
onion and fry until golden. Remove the onion with a slotted
spoon and stir into the meat mixture. Add the potato slices, a
few at a time, to the fat and fry until pale gold on each side.
Drain on kitchen paper.
3 Use any remaining melted fat to grease an ovenproof
casserole.
4 Half fill a large saucepan with water and bring to the boil.
Add the rice and salt and boil for 5 minutes. Drain, rinse with
cold water and drain again.
5 Sprinkle a little rice over the base of the casserole and then
cover with the minced meat. Arrange the potato slices over the
meat and then sprinkle with the cooked lentils, chickpeas or
peas. Spread the remaining rice evenly over the top. Dot the
surface with the pieces of butter or ghee and sprinkle in a few
tablespoons of water. Cover the casserole tightly and cook in
an oven preheated to 350°F, 180°C, Gas Mark 4, for 30–40
minutes. Remove from the oven and serve immediately.

Lucknow ki biryani – meat and kebabs in rice

The city of Lucknow came to prominence after the fall of the
Moghul Empire, when Delhi ceased to be the centre of North
Indian culture and arts. The Moghuls survived for a century or
more and with them flourished the new culinary culture of
Lucknow. This intricate dish is a good example of that rich era
in Indian history.

450g (1lb) lamb or beef, cut into 2.5cm (1") chunks
110g (4oz) ghee or butter
1 large onion, sliced
1 large onion, finely chopped
1 teaspoon fresh ginger, peeled and finely chopped
350g (12oz) long-grain rice, washed thoroughly under cold water and
   drained
1 teaspoon garam masala

Marinade:
1 teaspoon chilli pepper
½ teaspoon ginger
1 clove garlic, crushed
1 teaspoon salt
½ teaspoon cumin seeds, crushed
3–4 bruised cardamom pods
3–4 cloves
¼ teaspoon saffron dissolved in 2 tablespoons warm water
Juice of 1 small lemon

Kebab ingredients:
450g (1lb) minced lamb or beef
1 teaspoon salt
½ teaspoon ground cinnamon
½ teaspoon ground cardamom
1 clove garlic, crushed
½ teaspoon chilli pepper
1 tablespoon chopped fresh mint OR 1 teaspoon dried mint

Sauce:
150ml (¼ pint) yoghurt
2 tablespoons tomato purée
Water

Garnish:
1 tablespoon ghee or butter
1 tablespoon blanched almonds
1 tablespoon cashew nuts
1 tablespoon pistachio nuts, halved
2 tablespoons raisins or sultanas

1 Mix the marinade ingredients together in a large bowl, add
the meat cubes and rub the spices into them thoroughly. Set
aside for 2–3 hours.

2 Melt the ghee or butter in a large pan, add the sliced onion and fry until golden. Remove with a slotted spoon and reserve. Add the chopped onion to the pan and fry until golden. Add the chopped ginger and fry for a few seconds. Add the marinated meat with its spices and stir well. Fry for about 10 minutes, stirring frequently.

3 In a small bowl mix the yoghurt and tomato purée together and stir in 150ml (¼ pint) water. Pour into the saucepan and cover the pan. Cook over a low heat for about 30 minutes, stirring once or twice.

4 Meanwhile mix all the kebab ingredients together thoroughly until smooth. It will be easier to do this if you keep your hands damp with warm water. Form the mixture into small balls about 2.5cm (1″) in diameter.

5 When the meat cubes have been cooking for 30 minutes gently add the meatballs to the pan. Cook for 10–15 minutes, shaking the pan at intervals to turn them and to prevent sticking.

6 Add the rice and 450ml (¾ pint) water and sprinkle in the garam masala. Do not stir. Fit a lid on tightly and cook over a low heat for 20–30 minutes or until the rice is tender.

7 Just before serving melt the ghee or butter in a small pan and fry the nuts and raisins or sultanas until golden.

8 Spoon the biryani onto a large platter, sprinkle with the nut mixture and then with the reserved, fried onions.

Nasi goreng – fried rice with beef

Indonesian food may not be very subtle, but it is most assuredly fascinating, being full of contrasts in colour, flavours and textures. Coconut milk, lemon grass, peanut sauce, arak, tamarind, kemiri and kentjur are common ingredients. Since many of these are not readily available I have substituted them with those easier to find.

Nasi Goreng can be prepared with pork, but I have used the beef version. Another classic version 'Nasi Goreng Istimewa' incorporates crab or lobster meat as well as ham.

2 eggs
Salt and pepper
4 tablespoons vegetable or peanut oil
1 large onion, chopped
2 cloves garlic, crushed
½ teaspoon dried shrimp paste – sold in Chinese stores as 'Belachan'
1 teaspoon brown sugar
2 hot red chillis, chopped (optional)
1 tablespoon chopped coriander
1 teaspoon cumin
175g (6oz) prawns, de-veined
450g (1lb) lean beef steak, cut into 0.5cm (¼″) thin strips
350g (12oz) long-grain rice cooked as described on page 00
6 spring onions, thinly sliced
3 tablespoons soy sauce

Garnish:
thin cucumber slices

1 Beat the 2 eggs together in a small bowl with salt and
pepper to taste. Heat 1 tablespoon of the oil in a frying pan and
make an omelette with half of the egg mixture. Lift onto a
plate. Repeat the process with the remaining egg. When cool
place one omelette on top of the other, roll them up and cut into
thin strips. Reserve.
2 Heat the remaining oil in a large wok or frying pan. Add the
chopped onion and fry until golden. Remove with a slotted
spoon and drain on kitchen paper. In the remaining oil fry the
garlic, shrimp paste, sugar, chillis, coriander and cumin for
2–3 minutes, stirring constantly. Add the prawns and beef and
cook for 4–5 minutes. Stir in the cooked rice and spring onions
and fry until heated through. Add a little more oil if necessary.
Sprinkle in the soy sauce, mix thoroughly and spoon into a
large dish.
3 To serve garnish with cucumber slices and the omelette
strips and sprinkle with the fried onion.

Bokum bahb – crab and pork fried rice

'Transplanting rice,
he pissed
in a crony's field.' Yagu (1701–83) *Penguin Book of Zen Poetry*

A typically Korean (also Chinese) fried rice dish.

Crab can be substituted with other seafood such as prawns, lobster, white fish etc.; and the pork with beef, lamb, veal etc.

A simple dish to prepare.

5 tablespoons vegetable or peanut oil
2 cloves garlic, crushed
1½ teaspoons fresh ginger, peeled and grated
175g (6oz) flaked, cooked crab meat
225g (8oz) chopped, cooked pork
350g (12oz) long-grain rice prepared as in page 00
6 spring onions, thinly sliced

1 Heat the oil in a large wok or frying pan, add the garlic, ginger, crab meat and pork and fry, stirring constantly for 4–5 minutes. Add the rice and continue to fry for a further 3–4 minutes or until thoroughly heated through.
2 Mix in the spring onions and fry for a further 2–3 minutes. Serve immediately.

Kalbsreisfleisch – veal and rice casserole

The final recipes in this section are from Central Europe. The first is an old Austro-Hungarian dish and uses veal, while the second, from Hungary, makes use of sausage and sauerkraut.

75g (3oz) butter
3 tablespoons oil
3 medium onions, finely chopped
1kg (2lb) boned veal shoulder, cut into 2.5cm (1") cubes
2–3 tablespoons paprika
150ml (¼ pint) white wine
600ml (1 pint) stock or water
1 teaspoon salt
½ teaspoon black pepper
1 teaspoon dried thyme or oregano

350g (12oz) long-grain rice, washed thoroughly under cold water and
  drained

1 Heat the butter and oil in a large saucepan, add the onions
and fry until soft. Add the meat and fry, stirring frequently for
8–10 minutes.
2 Stir in the paprika, wine, stock or water, salt, pepper and
thyme or oregano. Bring to the boil, lower the heat, cover the
pan and simmer for about 45 minutes or until the meat is
tender.
3 Stir in the rice and a further 300ml (½ pint) water, cover the
pan and continue to simmer for a further 20–30 minutes or
until the rice is tender and the liquid absorbed.
4 Remove from the heat, leave for a few minutes and then
serve.

Kraut erdelya rakott kaposzta – sauerkraut with rice and sausage

1kg (2lb) sauerkraut
50g (2oz) butter or lard
2 large onions, finely chopped
1 clove garlic, crushed
450g (1lb) veal or pork, cut into 1cm (½″) pieces
225g (8oz) long-grain rice, washed under cold water thoroughly and
  drained
1 teaspoon salt
2 tablespoons paprika
225g (8oz) sausage of your choice, sliced
225g (8oz) thick bacon, cut into 1cm (½″) pieces
600ml (1 pint) yoghurt or soured cream

1 Place the sauerkraut in a large saucepan, cover with water
and bring to the boil. Simmer for 20 minutes and then drain.
2 Melt the butter in a saucepan, add the onions and fry until
soft. Add the garlic and pork and fry, stirring occasionally, for
about 20 minutes.
3 Meanwhile half fill a large saucepan with water and bring to
the boil. Add the rice and boil for 8 minutes. Remove from the
heat immediately and drain.

4 After the 20 minutes stir the salt, paprika, sausage and
bacon into the pork mixture and fry for a few more minutes.
5 Lightly grease a large, ovenproof casserole. Spread a third of
the sauerkraut over the base and arrange the meat mixture
over it. Cover with another third of the sauerkraut and then
spread evenly with the rice. Top with the remaining
sauerkraut and pour the yoghurt or soured cream over it.
6 Place in an oven preheated to 350°F, 180°C, Gas Mark 4 and
cook for 30 minutes. Remove from the oven and serve
immediately.

Rice with Chicken

The versatility of rice is unbounded. In this chapter it appears
with chicken, but it is equally good with other fowl e.g. goose,
poussins, duck, turkey, pigeons and other small birds. In North
Africa and other regions of the Middle East these small birds
include thrushes and swallows which are plucked, fried in oil
and cooked whole with rice and spices. One usually consumes
head, bones and all. Very delicious.

However, here we shall be mainly dealing with chicken. The
simplest way of cooking chicken with rice is shown in the
recipe below from Serbia (Yugoslavia). You can add your own
favourite herbs and spices and create new dishes.

Pileci risoto – chicken with rice

'Short supper – long life' – *Serbian proverb*

3 tablespoons oil
1 large onion, chopped
6 chicken portions OR 1 oven-ready chicken, cut into serving pieces
1 teaspoon salt
½–¾ teaspoon black pepper
1 tablespoon paprika
450g (1lb) tomatoes, blanched, peeled and quartered
450ml (¾ pint) boiling water or chicken stock

250g (9oz) long-grain rice, washed thoroughly under cold water and
   drained

1 Heat the oil in a large saucepan or casserole, add the onion
and fry until soft. Add the chicken pieces, salt, pepper and
paprika, lower the heat and fry for about 20 minutes, turning
frequently.
2 Add the tomatoes and half the water or stock, stir well, cover
and simmer for 30 minutes.
3 Meanwhile bring about 600ml (1 pint) of water to the boil in
a saucepan. Add the rice and simmer for 8 minutes. Drain
immediately.
4 Stir the par-boiled rice and the remaining water or stock
into the chicken pan. Cover the pan tightly and simmer until
the rice and chicken are tender.
5 Serve immediately.

Adas pollo ba morgh – lentils, rice and chicken

This is a delicious Iranian speciality.

250g (9oz) long-grain rice, washed thoroughly under cold water and
   drained
110g (4oz) green or continental lentils, washed thoroughly under cold
   water and drained
75g (3oz) butter
6 chicken portions OR 1 oven-ready chicken cut into serving pieces
1 large onion, chopped
1 teaspoon turmeric
450ml (¾ pint) water or stock
Juice 1 small lemon
1 tablespoon tomato purée
1 teaspoon salt
½ teaspoon black pepper
2 tablespoons raisins

1 Half fill two saucepans with lightly salted water and bring
to the boil. Place the rice in one and the lentils in the other and
boil for 10 minutes. Drain the rice, rinse with cold water and
set aside. Drain the lentils.

2 Melt half the butter in a flameproof casserole, add the
chicken pieces and fry until evenly browned. Remove from the
pan and set aside.
3 Add the onion to the pan and fry until soft and golden,
stirring frequently.
4 Stir in the turmeric, water or stock, lemon juice, tomato
purée, salt and pepper. Return the chicken pieces to the pan
and bring to the boil. Cover the pan and cook in an oven
preheated to 325°F, 170°C, Gas 3 for 1½ hours.
5 Remove from the oven. You can if you wish bone the chicken
pieces at this time.
6 Melt the remaining butter in a large saucepan and spread
half the rice over the base. Arrange the chicken pieces over it,
cover with the lentils and then sprinkle with the raisins. Spoon
half of the remaining chicken sauce over the top and then cover
with the remaining rice. Spread out evenly and spoon over
remaining chicken sauce.
7 Cover the pan with a tea towel and fix the lid on firmly. Lift
the ends of the tea towel up over the lid to prevent them
burning. Place over a low heat and steam for 30 minutes.
8 Serve straight from the pan.
   NB 'Ta-dig' is the Persian name for the crusty rice that will
form at the bottom of the pan (see page 16 – Kasmag pilav).
Cut this into wedges and serve separately.

Arroz a la filipina – glutinous rice and chicken

Malagkit is the Philippino name for glutinous rice (page 4)
and it is readily available from Chinese stores.
   Achuete (Bixa orellano) is the seed of the Arnotta tree and is
used in Philippino cooking as a colouring.

25g (1oz) butter
3 cloves garlic, crushed
1 onion, sliced
4 tomatoes, sliced
6 chicken portions OR 1 oven-ready chicken cut into serving pieces
1 teaspoon salt

½ teaspoon black pepper
600ml (1 pint) water
2 large green peppers, thinly sliced
Substitute achuete with 1 teaspoon turmeric OR ½ teaspoon saffron
  strands dissolved in a few tablespoons warm water
175g (6oz) glutinous rice, washed thoroughly under cold water and
  drained
175g (6oz) long-grain rice, washed thoroughly under cold water and
  drained
2 tablespoons raisins

Garnish:
2 hard-boiled eggs, quartered
fried bananas (see Glossary)

1 Melt the butter in a large saucepan and add the garlic, onion
and tomatoes. Fry for several minutes until soft.
2 Add the chicken pieces, salt and pepper and fry for several
minutes. Stir in the water and bring to the boil. Lower the
heat, cover the pan and simmer for 1 hour.
3 Add the sliced peppers and simmer for 2–3 minutes.
4 Stir in the turmeric or saffron and the two kinds of rice.
Cover and simmer over a low heat until the rice is tender.
5 Serve immediately on a large plate, garnished with
hard-boiled egg quarters, and fried bananas.

Arroz con pollo – Mexican chicken with rice

'Arroz', from the Arabic 'roz' (rice), arrived in the New World
via Spain. The Spanish conquistadors took with them, not only
their religion and language, but many of their culinary
traditions as they expanded their empire; hence the arroz
dishes of the Philippines.

   Arroz dishes are risottos, paellas or pollos. This particular
recipe, in one guise or another, appears throughout North and
South America, Portugal, Italy, North Africa and South-East
Asia.

   This is a simple and tasty dish. The Spaniards use saffron to
give the rice extra colour, but the Mexicans do not.

3 tablespoons oil
6 rashers bacon, rinds discarded, chopped
6 chicken portions OR 1 oven-ready chicken cut into serving pieces
3 tablespoons seasoned flour
1 large onion, chopped
2 cloves garlic, crushed
450g (1lb) tomatoes, blanched, peeled and chopped
1 large red pepper, thinly sliced
1 tablespoon paprika
250g (9oz) long-grain rice, washed thoroughly under cold water and
  drained
1 teaspoon salt
75g (3oz) peas
450ml (¾ pint) boiling water

Garnish:
2 tablespoons chopped parsley
Hot, cooked asparagus tips (optional)

1 Heat the oil in a large saucepan or casserole. Add the bacon
pieces and fry until crisp. Remove bacon with a slotted spoon,
drain on kitchen paper and set aside.
2 Coat the chicken pieces with the seasoned flour and fry,
three at a time, until lightly browned all over. Remove chicken
pieces from the pan and set aside.
3 Place the onion and garlic in the casserole and fry until soft,
stirring frequently to prevent sticking. Add the tomatoes, red
pepper and paprika and stir well. Return the chicken pieces to
the pan and turn to coat with the tomato mixture.
4 Cover the casserole and place in an oven preheated to 350°F,
180°C, Gas Mark 4. Cook for 40 minutes.
5 Remove from the oven and stir in the fried bacon, rice, salt,
peas and water. Cover, return to the oven and cook for a
further 30 minutes.
6 Serve straight from the casserole or turn into a serving dish.
Sprinkle with the garnish and serve.

West Indian chicken pilav

'You must have a couple grains of rice in order to catch fowls.' – You cannot trade without capital. *African expression*

An appealing mixture of rice, chicken, peas and sultanas all coated with a rich tomato and pepper mixture. In the true paella or risotto tradition.

120ml (4fl oz) oil
110g (4oz) sugar
6 large chicken pieces
2 onions, finely chopped
3 cloves garlic, crushed
2 green peppers, seeded and finely chopped
450g (1lb) tomatoes, blanched, peeled and chopped
2–3 green chillis, finely chopped
2 tablespoons capers (optional)
50g (2oz) sultanas or raisins
1 tablespoon chopped fresh thyme or 1½ teaspoons dried thyme
1 teaspoon salt
½ teaspoon black pepper
350g (12oz) long-grain rice, washed thoroughly under cold water and
  drained
300ml (½ pint) chicken stock or water, boiling
150ml (¼ pint) rum
225g (8oz) canned pigeon peas, drained

1 Heat the oil in a large saucepan or casserole. When the oil is hot lower the heat and add the sugar. Cook, stirring constantly until the sugar has melted and turned a dark brown.
2 Add the chicken pieces, two or three at a time and fry, turning frequently, until evenly browned. Transfer the pieces to a plate and set aside.
3 Add the onions, garlic and peppers and fry, stirring frequently, until the onions are soft.
4 Stir in the tomatoes, chillis, capers, sultanas, thyme, salt and pepper and cook over a low heat for 5 minutes, stirring frequently.
5 Return the chicken pieces to the pan, turn them to coat with the sauce, cover the pan and cook over a low heat for 30–40 minutes. Stir the ingredients occasionally.

6 Add the rice and stir in the stock or water and the rum and bring to the boil. Cover and simmer for 15–20 minutes or until the liquid has been absorbed and the rice is tender.

7 Stir in the pigeon peas and cook for a further 5 minutes or until they are heated through. Turn off the heat and leave for a few minutes before serving.

Risotto corine – rice with chicken and vegetables

A chicken and rice dish from the Low Countries.

6 rashers streaky bacon, cut into small pieces
75g (3oz) butter
4 chicken breasts, skinned, boned and cut into strips
2 onions, thinly sliced crossways and pushed out into rounds
2 large green peppers, seeded and coarsely chopped
1 stick celery, diced
225g (8oz) button mushrooms, wiped clean and halved
350g (12oz) long-grain rice, rinsed thoroughly under cold water and drained
450g (1lb) tomatoes, blanched, peeled and chopped
225g (8oz) sweetcorn
½ teaspoon dried thyme
1 teaspoon salt
½ teaspoon black pepper
¼ teaspoon chilli pepper
600ml (1 pint) boiling chicken stock
50g (2oz) grated parmesan cheese

1 Fry the bacon in a small non-stick frying pan until crisp. Remove with a slotted spoon and reserve.

2 Melt half the butter in a large saucepan, add the chicken strips and fry, stirring frequently, for 6–8 minutes or until evenly browned. Remove with a slotted spoon and set aside with the bacon.

3 Add the onions, peppers and celery to the pan and fry until soft, stirring frequently. Add the mushrooms and cook for a further 3 minutes. Remove the vegetables and set aside with the chicken and bacon.

4 Melt the remaining butter in the pan, add the rice and fry,

stirring constantly, for 3 minutes. Stir in the bacon, chicken, cooked vegetables, tomatoes, sweetcorn, thyme, salt, black pepper, chilli pepper and stock. Bring to the boil, stirring all the time. Cover the pan, lower the heat and simmer for about 20 minutes or until all the liquid has been absorbed and the rice is tender.

5 Pile into a large dish, sprinkle with the cheese and serve immediately.

Hav pilav – chicken pilav with peppers and yoghurt

A dish from Armenia which is often prepared with game such as partridge or pheasant.

300ml (½ pint) yoghurt
1 teaspoon turmeric
1 tablespoon coriander seeds, crushed
1 teaspoon paprika
3 tablespoons ground pistachios or pine kernels
½ teaspoon dried dillweed
1 teaspoon salt
3 tablespoons oil
1 onion, chopped
2 cloves garlic, crushed
6 chicken breasts
2 large green peppers, seeded and thinly sliced
2 large red peppers, seeded and thinly sliced
350g (12oz) long-grain rice, washed thoroughly under cold water and
    drained

Garnish:
1 teaspoon sumac powder
2 tablespoons chopped fresh tarragon or basil

1 In a bowl mix together the yoghurt, turmeric, coriander seeds, paprika, ground nuts, dillweed and salt and set aside.
2 Heat the oil in a large saucepan, add the onion and garlic and fry for a few minutes until soft. Add the chicken breasts and fry for about 5 minutes, turning occasionally.
3 Stir in the yoghurt mixture and the sliced peppers. Cover

the pan, lower the heat and simmer for 45 minutes, stirring
occasionally to prevent sticking.
4 Stir in the rice and add sufficient water to cover the rice and
chicken by 0.5cm (¼"). Bring to the boil, cover the pan tightly,
lower the heat and simmer for 15–20 minutes or until the
liquid has been absorbed and the rice is tender. Stir
occasionally to prevent sticking.
5 Turn off the heat and leave to 'rest' for 10 minutes. Turn into
a serving dish and sprinkle with the garnishes.

Bukara pollo – chicken pilav with herbs and spices

This Central Asian dish has many variations. Chicken is often
substituted with chunks of lamb or small lamb chops. In one
form or another it appears throughout Asia Minor, Iran and
the USSR. Sometimes sliced quinces or dried apricots are also
included.

The recipe below is a spicier version of the simple Uzbek
original. It comes from Kashmir in North India, hence the
'Indian' chillis, ginger, cinnamon and cardamom.

4–5 green chillis, thinly sliced
2 cloves garlic, crushed
1 teaspoon grated ginger
1 teaspoon cumin powder
6 tablespoons water
6 chicken breasts
3 tablespoons ghee or butter
1 large onion, thinly sliced
450g (1lb) tomatoes, blanched, peeled and chopped
350g (12oz) long-grain rice, washed thoroughly under cold water and
    drained
3 medium carrots, grated
1 small pomegranate, peeled and seeded
150ml (¼ pint) boiling water
1 teaspoon salt
5cm (2") cinnamon stick
3 cloves
3–4 cardamom pods

1 In a large bowl mix together the chillis, garlic, ginger, cumin and water. Add the chicken breasts and turn them several times until well coated. Cover the bowl and set aside for 2 hours.

2 Melt the ghee or butter in an ovenproof casserole. Add the onion and fry for a few minutes until soft. Add the chicken pieces, any remaining marinade and the tomatoes. Cover the pan and simmer over a low heat for 45 minutes.

3 Add all the remaining ingredients and stir well. Replace the lid. Place the casserole in an oven preheated to 350°F, 180°C, Gas Mark 4 and bake for 30 minutes or until all the liquid is absorbed and the rice is tender. Remove from the oven and leave to 'rest' for 10 minutes before serving.

Nasi megona – Indonesian chicken with vegetables and rice

One of the many Nasi (rice) dishes of Indonesia, which is not one land, but 3,000 islands. Doubtless there are as many 'Nasi' dishes scattered in the Indian Ocean.

The vegetables vary. Use what is available or preferred.

In this recipe the rice is cooked separately from the chicken and is not therefore a true pilav. However, the chicken-vegetable combination is so rich, tasty and different that I had to include it in this book.

A glorious and different dish.

350g (12oz) long-grain rice, washed thoroughly under cold water and
    drained
480ml (16fl oz) coconut milk
50g (2oz) grated fresh coconut OR desiccated coconut
225g (8oz) cabbage, sliced
225g (8oz) french beans, trimmed and cut into 5cm (2") pieces
10 button mushrooms, wiped clean and quartered
225g (8oz) peas
1 teaspoon coriander
¼ teaspoon *Laos* (root of Greater Galingale), omit if not available
¼ teaspoon *Serai* (Citronella Grass), omit if not available
600ml (1 pint) coconut milk
1 large onion, chopped
2 cloves garlic, crushed

6 chicken breasts
½ teaspoon shrimp paste (Belachan) or anchovy paste
1 level tablespoon brown sugar
2–3 bay leaves
1 teaspoon salt
1 tablespoon lemon juice

Garnish:
3 hard-boiled eggs, quartered
110g (4oz) unsalted peanuts fried in 2 teaspoons oil

1 Prepare the rice as described in 'Heen Pahb' (page 6) using the 480ml (16fl oz) of coconut milk instead of the water. When cooked set aside.
2 In a saucepan place the coconut milk, onion, garlic, chicken breasts, shrimp paste, sugar, bay leaves and salt. Stir well, cover the pan and simmer for about 1 hour, stirring occasionally.
3 Remove the lid, stir in the lemon juice and cook, uncovered for a further 5–10 minutes or until the sauce has thickened a little.
4 Meanwhile, place the grated or desiccated coconut, cabbage, beans, mushrooms, peas, coriander, *laos* and *serai* in the top part of a steamer and mix well. Cover, place on top of a pan of simmering water and steam for about 10 minutes or until the vegetables are cooked, but still crisp.
5 To serve: spread the rice over a large dish, make a well in the centre and arrange the chicken pieces in it and top with the vegetables. Garnish with the quartered eggs and fried peanuts.

Creole chicken Jambalaya

The best Jambalayas are cooked in the Southern United States, particularly in Louisiana. There are many so-called dishes made from meat and fish.
    Serve with a fresh salad of your choice.

6 tablespoons oil
3 tablespoons flour seasoned with ½ teaspoon salt and ¼ teaspoon black pepper

6 chicken portions
600ml (1 pint) stock or water
1 teaspoon salt
½ teaspoon black pepper
½ teaspoon chilli pepper
3 bacon rashers, chopped
1 large onion, chopped
1 clove garlic, crushed
1 large green pepper, seeded and thinly sliced
4 medium tomatoes, blanched, peeled and chopped
2 celery sticks, trimmed and chopped
350g (12oz) long-grain rice, washed thoroughly under cold water and
   drained
2 bay leaves

Garnish:
2 tablespoons finely chopped parsley

1 Heat half the oil in a large pan.
2 Spread the seasoned flour on a plate and coat the chicken
pieces with it. Place them in the pan, two or three at a time,
and fry, turning occasionally, until evenly browned.
3 Add the stock or water, salt, black pepper and chilli pepper
and bring to the boil. Cover the pan, lower the heat and
simmer for 1 hour.
4 Meanwhile heat the remaining oil in another pan, add the
bacon pieces and fry for 5 minutes or until crisp and browned.
Remove with a slotted spoon and drain on kitchen paper. Add
the onion and garlic to the pan and fry until soft. Stir in the
green pepper, tomatoes and celery and fry for a further 2–3
minutes. Stir in the rice and bay leaves.
5 Tip the vegetable and rice mixture into the chicken pan. Add
the bacon pieces and stir thoroughly. Cover the pan and
continue to simmer for about 20 minutes or until the liquid has
been absorbed and the rice is tender. Remove from the heat
and leave to 'rest' for 10 minutes.
6 Transfer the Jambalaya to a large serving dish, sprinkle
with the parsley and serve.

Picardy rice – rice with chicken, tomatoes and bacon

6 rashers streaky bacon, diced
50g (2oz) butter
4 chicken breasts, skinned, boned and cut into thin strips
1 onion, chopped
2 green peppers, seeded thinly sliced
450g (1lb) tomatoes, blanched, peeled and chopped
1½ teaspoon salt
½ teaspoon black pepper
½ teaspoon dried thyme
½ teaspoon dried oregano
350g (12oz) long-grain rice, washed thoroughly under cold water and
  drained
450ml (¾ pint) boiling stock or water

1 In a small, non-stick frying pan fry the bacon until it is crisp.
Scrape the bottom frequently with a wooden spoon to prevent
sticking. Remove from the heat, transfer the bacon to kitchen
paper with a slotted spoon and reserve.
2 Melt the butter in a large saucepan, add the chicken strips
and fry for 7–10 minutes, stirring frequently. Remove with a
slotted spoon and set aside.
3 Add the onion and green peppers to the pan and fry until
soft. Add the tomatoes, salt, pepper, thyme, oregano, fried
chicken and rice. Stir well and fry for 2–3 minutes.
4 Stir in the boiling water or stock. Cover the pan, lower the
heat and simmer for about 20 minutes or until the liquid has
been absorbed and the rice is tender. Turn off the heat and set
aside to 'rest' for 10 minutes.
5 Spoon the pilav into a large serving dish, sprinkle with the
fried bacon and serve.

Risotto al fegato di pollo – chicken liver risotto

A very tasty and inexpensive dish which is simple to prepare.

75g (3oz) butter
1 large onion, finely chopped
225g (8oz) mushrooms, wiped clean and sliced

350g (12oz) long-grain rice, washed thoroughly under cold water and
  drained
1 teaspoon salt
720ml (24fl oz) boiling water or chicken stock
12 chicken livers, cut into small pieces
3 tablespoons finely chopped parsley

Garnish:
75g (3oz) grated parmesan cheese (optional)

1 Melt 50g (2oz) of the butter in a large pan. Add the onion and
fry, stirring occasionally, until soft and turning golden. Add
the mushrooms and fry for a further 2–3 minutes.
2 Add the rice and fry for 2 minutes, stirring frequently. Add
the salt and water or stock and boil vigorously for 1 minute.
Cover the pan, lower the heat and simmer for 15–20 minutes
or until the liquid has been absorbed.
3 Meanwhile melt the remaining butter in a small pan, add
the pieces of chicken liver and fry for 5–8 minutes, stirring
frequently.
4 When the rice is cooked, stir in the chicken livers and
parsley and set aside 'to rest' for 10 minutes.
5 To serve spoon the pilav into a large dish and sprinkle with
the cheese.

Albaloo pollo – chicken with rice and cherries

For this brilliant Iranian dish you really need sour cherries
which, unfortunately are not readily available. However, do
not despair for cherries bottled or tinned in a light syrup or
natural juice make an excellent substitute.

3 tablespoons oil
150ml (¼ pint) water
1 tablespoon tomato purée
½ teaspoon turmeric
Juice 1 lemon
1 teaspoon salt
½ teaspoon black pepper
1.75–2.25kg (4–5lb) oven-ready chicken
1 tablespoon salt

350g (12oz) long-grain rice, washed thoroughly under cold water and
  drained
450g (1lb) sour fresh cherries OR bottled morello cherries
sugar (see recipe)
2 tablespoons butter

Garnish:
1 tablespoon butter
2 tablespoons slivered almonds
2 tablespoons slivered pistachios

1 In a bowl mix together the oil, water, tomato purée,
turmeric, lemon juice, salt and black pepper. Pour into a large
casserole, add the whole chicken and turn to coat with the
mixture. Bake in an oven preheated to 350°F, 180°C, Gas Mark
4 for about 1½ hours, basting regularly.
2 Meanwhile half fill a large saucepan with water, add the
tablespoon of salt and bring to the boil. Add the rice and boil
for 5 minutes. Drain immediately and reserve.
3 If using fresh sour cherries, stone them and place in a pan
with 1kg (2lb) sugar and 4–5 tablespoons water. Simmer for
20–30 minutes, stirring regularly until the mixture is thick.
Remove from the heat.
   If using bottled cherries, drain them and remove the stones.
Place the cherries in a pan, add 225g (8oz) sugar and 4–5
tablespoons water and simmer, stirring frequently, until the
mixture thickens. Remove from the heat.
4 When the chicken is cooked remove from the oven, leave to
cool and then skin and bone it. Cut the flesh into smaller
pieces.
5 Melt the butter in a large ovenproof casserole. Spread half
the rice over the base and spoon over half the cherry mixture.
Arrange the chicken pieces evenly over the top and then cover
with the remaining cherry mixture. Spread the rest of the rice
evenly over the cherries. Sprinkle with 4–5 tablespoons of
water and cover the casserole. Bake in an oven preheated to
350°F, 180°C, Gas Mark 4 for 25–30 minutes.
6 Meanwhile prepare the garnish by melting the butter in a
small pan. Add the nuts and fry, stirring frequently until
golden.

7 Remove the casserole from the oven, sprinkle with the nuts and serve with a salad.

Khusbudar pilao – chicken with fruit and nuts

'Friends are rice-stores' – *Kashmiri saying*

A glorious, colourful dish from Northern India. Serve with dhunia chutney, raita (page 00) and a bowl of mixed salad.

1 teaspoon salt
4 dried chillis, pulverised OR 2 teaspoons chilli pepper
½ teaspoon crushed cardamom
6 chicken pieces
4 tablespoons oil
4 large carrots, peeled and thinly sliced
2 tablespoons slivered almonds
2 tablespoons slivered pistachios
1 teaspoon fresh ginger, grated
1 clove garlic, crushed
1 large onion, thinly sliced
5cm (2″) stick cinnamon
1 teaspoon ground cumin
rind of 1 orange, white pith discarded, thinly sliced
juice 1 orange
50g (2oz) mixed sultanas and raisins
350g (12oz) long-grain rice, washed thoroughly under cold water and
  drained
600ml (1 pint) boiling water
¼ teaspoon powdered saffron dissolved in 2 tablespoons warm milk

1 Mix the salt, chillis or chilli pepper and cardamom with 2–3 tablespoons water. Rub this paste into the chicken pieces and set aside for 2 hours.
2 In a large pan heat half the oil, add the carrot slices and fry for about 5 minutes, stirring regularly. Remove with a slotted spoon, drain on kitchen paper and reserve.
3 Add the nuts and fry, stirring frequently, until golden. Remove with a slotted spoon, drain on kitchen paper and reserve.
4 Add the remaining oil to the pan, add the ginger, garlic,

onion, cinnamon stick and cumin and fry, stirring frequently until the onion is soft. Stir in half the orange peel and chicken pieces and turn to coat with the spices. Add the orange juice, cover the pan tightly and simmer over a low heat for 45–60 minutes, stirring occasionally.

5 Stir in the mixed fruit, rice, nuts, carrots and water. Cover the pan and simmer for about 20 minutes or until all the liquid has been absorbed. After 10 minutes of the cooking time remove the lid and stir in the saffron mixture and then replace the lid and continue cooking.

6 Meanwhile in a small saucepan bring 300ml (½ pint) water to the boil, add the remaining orange peel and simmer for 5 minutes. Remove from the heat and drain.

7 When the rice is cooked remove from the heat and leave the pilav to 'rest' for 10 minutes. Spoon the pilav into a large serving dish and sprinkle with the reserved orange peel.

Juja plov doshyamya – chicken with rice, pumpkin and chestnuts

This uniquely-flavoured dish hails from Azerbaijan, USSR, in the Caucasus and is typical of the entire mountainous region of the Southern Soviet Union. Lamb can be substituted for the chicken, as can beef, minced meat or meatballs. If you cannot find fresh chestnuts use tinned ones. In this case there is no need to shell or skin them, simply drain and use.

1 tablespoon salt
350g (12oz) long-grain rice, washed thoroughly under cold water and
  drained
175g (6oz) chestnuts
75g (3oz) butter
75g (3oz) raisins
8 dried prunes, stoned and halved
8 dried apricots, quartered
½ teaspoon sugar
½ teaspoon cinnamon
350g (12oz) pumpkin, peeled and cut into 5 × 1cm (2″ × ½″) pieces
4 boned chicken breasts, cut into 1cm (½″) pieces

1 teaspoon salt
½ teaspoon black pepper
4 tablespoons melted butter

Garnish:
1 tablespoon sumac powder

1 Half fill a large saucepan with water, add the salt and bring
to the boil. Add the rice in a steady stream and boil for 5
minutes. Drain immediately and set aside.
2 If using fresh chestnuts slit each one halfway around with a
sharp knife. Place them in a saucepan, cover with water and
bring to the boil. Simmer for 5 minutes and then remove from
the heat. Lift the chestnuts out with a slotted spoon and shell
and skin them quickly while still warm. Reserve.
3 Melt half the butter in a large frying pan, add the dried
fruits, sugar and cinnamon and fry for 3–4 minutes, stirring
frequently with a wooden spoon. Remove with a slotted spoon,
drain on kitchen paper and reserve.
4 Melt half the remaining butter in the pan, add the chestnuts
and fry for 3–4 minutes, stirring constantly, until lightly
browned. Remove, drain on kitchen paper and reserve with the
fruits.
5 Add the remaining butter and the pumpkin pieces to the pan
and fry, turning carefully, until well browned. Remove with a
slotted spoon and reserve with the fruits and chestnuts.
6 Add the chicken pieces to the pan and fry for about 10
minutes, turning frequently. Add a little more butter if
necessary. Remove with a slotted spoon and reserve.
7 Brush a large saucepan or casserole with 2 tablespoons of
the melted butter. Arrange half the rice over the base, top with
the chicken pieces and sprinkle with the salt and pepper.
Spread the fruit, chestnut and pumpkin mixture evenly over
the chicken and then cover with the remaining rice. Sprinkle
the 2 remaining tablespoons of melted butter over the top.
8 Cover the top with a tea towel and then fit a lid on tightly.
Lift the edges of the tea towel up onto the lid to prevent them
burning. Steam over a very low heat for 30 minutes.
9 Serve garnished with the sumac.

Riszes libaaprolek – goose with rice and mushrooms

Goose is still very popular throughout Europe and the
Balkans. Indeed, in most European lands it is still the
Christmas fare. This recipe is from Hungary, but rice with
goose appears throughout the region and as far away as the
Caucasus.

1 medium goose, trimmed of all fat, cut into serving pieces
1 large onion, quartered
3 tablespoons fat or butter
250g (9oz) long-grain rice, washed thoroughly under cold water and
  drained
175g (6oz) mushrooms, wiped clean and thinly sliced
4 tablespoons parsley
½ teaspoon marjoram
1 teaspoon salt
1 teaspoon paprika
½ teaspoon black pepper

Garnish:
1 tablespoon butter or fat
110g (4oz) goose liver, chopped

1 Place the goose pieces in a large pan with the quartered
onion. Cover with water and bring to the boil. Lower the heat
and simmer for 45–60 minutes or until the goose is tender.
Remove any scum that appears on the surface. When cooked
discard the onion.
2 Melt the fat or butter in a large pan, add the rice and
mushrooms and fry for 2–3 minutes, stirring frequently. Stir
in the parsley and all the seasonings.
3 Add the goose pieces and 600ml (1 pint) of the goose stock.
Mix well and bring quickly to the boil. Lower the heat, cover
and simmer for about 20 minutes or until the liquid has been
absorbed and the rice is tender.
4 To prepare the garnish melt the butter or fat in a small pan,
add the pieces of goose liver and fry for 5–10 minutes, stirring
frequently.
5 Transfer the goose and rice to a large dish, sprinkle with the
fried liver and serve.

Variation: Gaz kavourma plov – goose and prune pilav

Follow the above recipe but:
1 incorporate 110g (4oz) stoned, dried prunes, halved, at the same time as you fry the rice. You can omit the mushrooms if you wish.
2 Dissolve ½ teaspoon powdered saffron in 2 tablespoons warm water and add to the rice with the rest of the seasonings.

Rice with Fish and Shellfish

'Rice, fish and cucumber are born in water, but die in wine.'
– *Portuguese expression*

Think of rice and fish and one immediately conjures up the vision of those colourful, rich dishes of Spain – paellas – truely one of the glories of Iberian cooking. The name 'paella' comes from the dish in which the rice is cooked and served. It is traditionally a flat, oval, earthenware pan with two handles.

Paella-named dishes appear throughout South and Central America and the Philippines. They are all inspired by Spain, the Mother Country. 'Arroz', 'risotto' and 'pilau' are all basically the same i.e. rice, fish and vegetables with herbs and spices. There are countless such dishes and often pork, chicken and other meats are incorporated.

The first recipe is a typical 'paella' served in most Spanish or Portuguese restaurants. It is followed by variations from Portugal, Spain and other lands.

Paella – Spanish rice with seafood and chicken

'Chorizo' is a sausage which contains lean beef, lean and fat pork, red peppers and marjoram. It is sold in some continental shops and large supermarkets. You can substitute Italian 'pepperoni' sausage or any spicy continental sausage of your choice.

4 tablespoons oil
1 large onion, thinly sliced
2 cloves garlic, crushed
6 chicken pieces
1 large red pepper, seeded and chopped
225g (8oz) tomatoes, blanched, peeled and chopped
1½ teaspoons salt
½ teaspoon black pepper
1 teaspoon paprika
1 chorizo sausage, sliced
225g (8oz) peas
350g (12oz) long-grain rice, washed thoroughly under cold water and
  drained
450ml (¾ pint) boiling water
Juice 1 lemon
¼ teaspoon saffron, dissolved in 2 tablespoons warm water
25g (1oz) butter
110g (4oz) large prawns or shrimps
Flesh of 1 large, cooked lobster, cut into bite-sized pieces (reserve
  shells for garnish)
12 mussels, scrubbed, steamed and removed from their shells

Garnish:
2 tablespoons finely chopped parsley

1 Heat the oil in a very large, deep frying pan or casserole.
Add the onion and garlic and fry until soft. Add the chicken
pieces and fry until evenly browned. Stir in the red pepper,
tomatoes, salt, pepper, paprika and chorizo. Cover the pan and
simmer over a low heat for 30–45 minutes, stirring
occasionally.
2 Stir in the peas and rice. Mix the boiling water, lemon juice
and dissolved saffron and pour into the pan. Mix well, cover
and simmer over a low heat until all the liquid has been
absorbed.
3 Meanwhile melt the butter in a small pan, add shrimps or
prawns, lobster meat and mussels and fry for 4–5 minutes.
Remove with a slotted spoon and arrange over the paella for
the last 5–10 minutes of its cooking time. Turn off the heat and
leave for a few minutes. Sprinkle with the parsley and serve.

Arroz a la Valenciana – Valencian-style paella

This is the most famous Spanish rice dish that is cooked in a 'paellera'.

Chicken, beef, lobster, ham, sausage, mussels, peas etc. are all mixed together to make a magnificent dish.

Serve with a bowl of salad.

5 tablespoons oil
1 large onion, chopped
2 cloves garlic, crushed
1 large red pepper, seeded and thinly sliced
4 tomatoes, blanched, peeled and chopped
6 chicken pieces
225g (8oz) steak, cut into 1cm (½") pieces
110g (4oz) thick ham, cut into small cubes
1 chorizo sausage, thinly sliced
175g (6oz) peas
1½ teaspoons salt
½ teaspoon black pepper
1 teaspoon paprika
350g (12oz) long-grain rice, washed thoroughly under cold water and drained
450ml (¾ pint) boiling water
¼ teaspoon saffron dissolved in 2 tablespoons warm water
25g (1oz) butter
225g (8oz) hake, cut into small chunks
Flesh of 1 cooked lobster, cut into bite-sized pieces
225g (8oz) shrimps
12 mussels, scrubbed, steamed and removed from their shells

Garnish:
1 red pepper, seeded and thinly sliced

1 Heat the oil in a large, deep frying pan or casserole. Add the onion, garlic and red pepper and fry until soft, stirring occasionally. Stir in the tomatoes and chicken pieces, cover the pan and simmer for 30–45 minutes, stirring occasionally.
2 Add the steak, ham, sausage, peas, seasonings and rice and fry for 5 minutes, stirring frequently. Stir in the water and saffron liquid, cover the pan and simmer over a low heat until all the liquid has been absorbed.

3 Meanwhile melt the butter in a frying pan, add the pieces of hake and fry for about 5 minutes, stirring frequently. Add the lobster, shrimps and mussels and fry for a further 5 minutes, still stirring regularly. Remove the fish with a slotted spoon and stir into the cooking paella. When all the liquid has been absorbed, turn off the heat, leave for a few minutes and then garnish with the strips of red pepper and serve.

Arroz de camarao – rice with prawns, Portuguese-style

Rice with prawns or shrimps, in one version or another, appears all over the world. However, very few can equal the simplicity of this dish from Southern Portugal.

1 large carrot, peeled and chopped
2 onions, chopped
1 sprig parsley
2 bay leaves
900ml (1½ pints) water
1 teaspoon salt
½ teaspoon black pepper
225g (8oz) prawns
3 tablespoons oil
350g (12oz) long-grain rice, washed thoroughly under cold water and
  drained
1½ tablespoons tomato purée
25g (1oz) butter

1 Place the chopped carrot, one of the chopped onions, the parsley, bay leaves, water, salt and black pepper in a saucepan and bring to the boil. Lower the heat and simmer for 15 minutes. Add 150g (5oz) of the prawns and cook for 2 minutes. Turn off the heat and discard the bay leaves.
2 Transfer the mixture to a blender and reduce to a smooth cream. If necessary make this stock up to 720ml (24fl oz) with water.
3 Heat the oil in a saucepan, add the remaining chopped onion and fry until soft. Stir in the rice and tomato purée and fry for 1–2 minutes. Add the puréed stock and bring to the boil. Lower

the heat and simmer for 20 minutes or until all the liquid has
been absorbed. Stir occasionally. Turn off the heat.
4 Meanwhile melt the butter in a small pan, add the
remaining prawns and fry for 3–4 minutes. Stir this mixture
into the pilav and leave to 'rest' for 10 minutes before serving.

Risotto con gamberetti – Italian rice with shrimps

A typical risotto which is filling, tasty and colourful.

You can use Italian Avouo rice, but long-grain rice is equally
good.

If fresh shrimps are available do use them. Drop in boiling
water for 1 minute and then peel. Otherwise frozen ones will
do.

110g (4oz) butter
1 large onion, thinly sliced
2 cloves garlic, crushed
175g (6oz) button mushrooms, wiped clean and sliced
½ teaspoon dried basil
1 teaspoon salt
½ teaspoon black pepper
350g (12oz) long-grain rice, washed thoroughly under cold water and
  drained
120ml (4fl oz) dry white wine
600ml (1 pint) water or stock
450g (1lb) shrimps
½ teaspoon saffron dissolved in 2 tablespoons warm water
50g (2oz) grated parmesan cheese

1 Melt 75g (3oz) of the butter in a large saucepan, add the
onion and garlic and fry until soft, stirring occasionally. Add
the mushrooms, basil, salt and black pepper and fry for a
further 2–3 minutes. Add the rice and stir until all the grains
are well coated with butter.
2 Stir in the wine and water and bring to the boil. Lower the
heat, cover and simmer for 15 minutes. Remove the lid, stir in
the shrimps with a fork, re-cover and cook for a further 5
minutes or until all the liquid has been absorbed. Finally stir

in the dissolved saffron, remaining butter and the cheese. Turn off the heat, leave to 'rest' for a few minutes and then serve.

Jhingo pilav – curried rice with shrimps

'I have offered water in a brass pot,
I have offered gruel in a leaf-cup.
I have served him rice in a dish,
I have given him curry in a leaf-cup,
But he does not speak to me.' – *Indian folk song 'Unwritten Song'*

A delicious shrimp and vegetable pilav with a tasty sauce.

450g (1lb) peeled prawns or shrimps
1 teaspoon salt
1 level teaspoon chilli pepper
juice 1 lemon

Pilav:
50g (2oz) butter or ghee
1 large onion, thinly sliced
2 cloves garlic, crushed
1 teaspoon cumin seeds
1 teaspoon turmeric
110g (4oz) french beans, trimmed and halved
2 large carrots, peeled and sliced into thin rounds
2 small courgettes, sliced into thin rounds
350g (12oz) long-grain rice, washed thoroughly under cold water and
    drained
600ml (1 pint) boiling water

Sauce:
3 tablespoons oil
1 onion, chopped
1 clove garlic, crushed
5cm (2″) piece ginger, peeled and chopped
2 green chillis, seeded and finely chopped
1 tablespoon ground coriander
2 teaspoons paprika
675g (1½lb) tomatoes, blanched, peeled, chopped and rubbed through
    a sieve
1 teaspoon salt

2 teaspoons brown sugar
2 tablespoons coconut milk (see page 227)

1 Place the shrimps on a large plate, rub in the salt, chilli
pepper and lemon juice and set aside.
2 To prepare the pilav melt the butter in a large saucepan, add
the onion and garlic and fry until soft. Add the cumin, turmeric
and all the vegetables and stir thoroughly. Cover the pan,
lower the heat and fry for 10–12 minutes, stirring occasionally.
Mix in the rice and fry for 2–3 minutes. Add the shrimps and
their marinade and stir in gently. Pour in the boiling water,
cover the pan and simmer gently until all the liquid has been
absorbed. Set aside to 'rest' for a few minutes.
3 Meanwhile prepare the sauce by heating the oil in a
saucepan. Add the onion, garlic, ginger and chillis and fry for
about 5 minutes, stirring frequently. Add the coriander,
paprika, strained tomato, salt and sugar. Stir well and bring
quickly to the boil. Cover the pan, lower the heat and simmer
for about 20 minutes. Stir in the coconut milk, simmer for a
few minutes and remove from the heat.
4 To serve, transfer the pilav to a large dish. Either pour the
sauce over the pilav or serve in a separate sauceboat.

Kedgeree (khitcheri)

The classic khitcheri dishes – of which there are many
throughout India – are basically rice and lentil fare, tasty,
simple and cheap. Kedgeree is the Anglo-Indian name, given
to those same dishes, which the empire-builders brought back
with them and which they then developed to suit their British
palates. What did they do? They added vegetables, meat,
chicken and especially fish. In fact today there must be as
many kedgeree dishes as there are ex Anglo-Indians! I have
included two such fish kedgerees. Always serve with khuri
(page 220) if you wish to be authentic.

Haddock kedgeree

110g (4oz) butter
450g (1lb) cooked, smoked haddock, skinned, boned and flaked
350g (12oz) cooked rice (page 5)
3 hard-boiled eggs, shelled and chopped
1 teaspoon salt
½ teaspoon black pepper
½ teaspoon chilli pepper
3 tablespoons single cream

Garnish:
2 tablespoons finely chopped parsley

1 Melt 75g (3oz) of the butter in a large frying pan. Add the
flaked fish, rice, chopped eggs, salt, black pepper and chilli
pepper and mix gently, but thoroughly. Stir in the cream and
heat through for 5–10 minutes. Stir occasionally.
2 Transfer to a large dish, sprinkle with the parsley and dot
with the remaining butter. Serve with salad and khuri (page
220).

Salmon kedgeree

675g (1½lb) fresh salmon, cut into steaks
25g (1oz) butter
40g (1½oz) plain flour
150ml (¼ pint) milk
300ml (½ pint) fish stock
1 level teaspoon salt
½ teaspoon black pepper
3 whole cloves
½ teaspoon grated nutmeg
¼ teaspoon cinnamon
50g (2oz) butter
1 onion, finely chopped
2 teaspoons curry powder
350g (12oz) cooked rice (see page 5)
3 hard-boiled eggs, finely chopped

1 Place the salmon steaks in a large pan and cover with water.
Bring to the boil, lower the heat and simmer for about 30

minutes or until the fish is tender. Transfer the fish to a large
plate and reserve the stock. When cool enough to handle
remove the skin and bones and flake the salmon.

2 Prepare a sauce by melting the 25g (1oz) butter in a medium
pan. Stir in the flour and cook, stirring constantly for 1–2
minutes. Gradually stir in the milk until the sauce is smooth.
Add 300ml (½ pint) of the fish stock and bring to a boil over a
low heat, stirring constantly until the sauce has thickened.
Season with the salt, pepper, cloves, nutmeg and cinnamon.
Gently stir in the flaked salmon and cook over a very low heat
for 5–7 minutes.

3 Meanwhile melt the 50g (2oz) of butter in a large saucepan,
add the onion and fry until soft. Stir in the curry powder and
then add the cooked rice and half the chopped eggs and mix
thoroughly. Add the salmon mixture and stir into the rice.
Cover the pan and heat over a low heat for 5–10 minutes,
stirring gently from time to time.

4 Transfer to a large dish, sprinkle with the remaining
chopped egg and serve immediately.

Balig plov – pilav with fish and dried fruit

This is a typical Caucasian dish enriched with apricots, raisins
and fresh grapes.

350g (12oz) cooked rice, incorporating ½ teaspoon saffron diluted in
  2 tablespoons hot water
225g (8oz) seedless white grapes
110g (4oz) butter
1 large onion, chopped
1kg (2lb) halibut, or other firm white fish, flesh cut into 2.5cm
  (1″) chunks
110g (4oz) dried apricots, chopped
110g (4oz) raisins
1 teaspoon salt
½ teaspoon dillweed

1 Prepare the rice as described on page 5, stirring in grapes
5 minutes before end of the cooking time.

2 Meanwhile melt 50g (2oz) of the butter in a large pan, add

the onion and fry until soft. Remove the onion with a slotted spoon and reserve.

3 Melt the remaining butter in the pan, add the fish and fry 5–7 minutes, stirring frequently. Return the cooked onion and add the apricots, raisins, salt, pepper and dillweed. Mix together gently and add 150ml (¼ pint) water. Cover the pan and simmer for 15 minutes.

4 To serve arrange the rice around the edge of a large dish and pile the fish and fruit mixture into the centre.

Trabzon hamsi tavasi – anchovy and rice pilav

The region of Trabzon is on the North-East coastline of Turkey. The cuisine is rich with fish dishes, and a particular favourite is anchovy. Indeed, the entire populace is often called 'Anchovy's children'.

This rice and fish dish is a classic. Make sure you use fresh anchovies, which are usually available at good fishmongers.

Serve with salads.

1kg (2lb) fresh anchovies, cleaned and de-boned
4 tablespoons salt
75g (3oz) butter
1 large onion, chopped
350g (12oz) long-grain rice, washed thoroughly under cold water and
   drained
720ml (24fl oz) boiling water
3 tablespoons pine kernels OR blanched slivered almonds OR halved
   hazelnuts
2 teaspoons sugar
2 tablespoons sultanas
¾ teaspoon allspice
1½ teaspoons salt
¾ teaspoon cinnamon
½ teaspoon black pepper

Garnish:
½ teaspoon dillweed
1 teaspoon paprika
1 tablespoon sumac, optional

1 Place the anchovies in a large dish in a single layer and
sprinkle with the salt. Set aside.
2 Melt 50g (2oz) of the butter in a large saucepan, add the
onion and fry until soft. Add the rice and cook for a few
minutes, stirring frequently. Add the water, nuts, sugar,
sultanas, allspice, salt, cinnamon and black pepper and stir
well. Boil vigorously for 1 minute then lower the heat, cover
the pan and simmer for about 20 minutes or until all the liquid
has been absorbed.
3 Rinse the anchovies thoroughly under cold water and dry
with kitchen paper.
4 Grease a large casserole dish and arrange half of them in a
single layer over the base. Spread the rice mixture over them
evenly and then arrange the remaining anchovies over the top.
5 Melt the remaining butter and sprinkle over the fish. Cover
the dish and cook in an oven preheated to 375°F, 190°C, Gas
Mark 5 for 15–20 minutes or until the fish are cooked.
6 Remove from the oven and sprinkle with the garnishes.
Serve hot.

Sayyadiyah – Arab fish and rice pilav

This is particularly popular in Syria and Lebanon.
    Any white fish will do. I have suggested halibut, but cod,
hake, salmon etc. are equally successful.
    Serve with a bowl of fresh salad.

2 tablespoons butter
1kg (2lb) halibut steaks, each one cut in half
2 tablespoons lemon juice
½ teaspoon salt
¼ teaspoon black pepper
2 tablespoons finely chopped parsley
6 tablespoons oil
1 onion, finely chopped
2 tablespoons pine kernels
2 tablespoons sultanas or raisins
½ teaspoon allspice
350g (12oz) cooked rice incorporating ½ teaspoon saffron diluted in
    2 tablespoons hot water

2 tablespoons lemon juice
2 tablespoons finely chopped parsley
1 teaspoon salt
½ teaspoon black pepper

Sauce:
4 tablespoons oil
1 tablespoon pine kernels
1 tablespoon dried mint
1 tablespoon lemon juice
½ teaspoon cumin

1 Melt half the butter in a large, shallow baking dish and add
the pieces of fish. Sprinkle with the lemon juice, salt, pepper
and chopped parsley. Dot the remaining butter over the fish
and then bake in an oven preheated to 325°F, 160°C, Gas Mark
3 for about 30 minutes or until the fish is cooked.
2 Remove from the oven, leave to cool and then flake the fish
and remove and discard the bones. Set the flaked fish aside.
3 Heat the oil in a large saucepan, add the onion and fry until
soft. Add the pine kernels, sultanas or raisins, allspice, cooked
saffron rice, lemon juice, parsley, salt and pepper. Mix all these
ingredients together carefully.
4 Spread half the rice mixture over the base of a large
ovenproof dish. Arrange half the reserved fish over the rice.
Cover with the remaining rice and top with the rest of the fish.
5 Prepare the sauce by heating the oil in a small pan. Add all
the ingredients and fry for a few minutes, until the nuts are
golden, stirring frequently. Pour this sauce evenly over the
surface of the casserole and bake in an oven preheated to
375°F, 190°C, Gas Mark 5 for about 15–20 minutes or until the
dish is heated through. Remove and serve immediately.

Ikan bryani – Malay spiced fish pilav

'Eating my morning rice,
I hold my bowl in the palm of my hand.
I do not eat, I think of her,
I hold my chopsticks ready,
But instead of picking up vegetables, I think of her.'
                    Song of a young man about to be married. 'Unwritten Song'

Malay cooking reflects the mixture of her inhabitants – native Malay, Chinese, Indian, Indonesian and Sri Lankan. This recipe has a strong Indonesian flavour about it.

1kg (2lb) fillets or steaks white fish, bones and skin discarded
Juice 1 lemon
1 teaspoon salt
¼ teaspoon black pepper
½ teaspoon turmeric
2 tablespoons ghee or butter
1 onion, finely chopped
3–4 whole cardamom pods, slightly bruised
3 whole cloves
5cm (2″) piece cinnamon
350g (12oz) long-grain rice, washed thoroughly under cold water and
  drained
600ml (1 pint) boiling water
1 teaspoon salt
90ml (3fl oz) oil
1 large onion, chopped
2 cloves garlic, crushed
1½ teaspoons grated fresh ginger
3 teaspoons ground coriander
2 teaspoons cumin
225g (½lb) tomatoes, blanched, peeled and chopped
150ml (¼ pint) water
150ml (¼ pint) coconut milk (page 227)

1 Cut the fish into 2.5cm (1″) pieces and arrange on a large plate. Sprinkle with the lemon juice, salt, pepper and turmeric and set aside for 10–15 minutes.
2 Meanwhile prepare the pilav by melting the ghee or butter in a saucepan. Add the onion and fry until soft. Add the cardamom, cloves, cinnamon and rice and fry for 2–3 minutes, stirring frequently. Stir in the water and salt and boil vigorously for 1 minute. Lower the heat, cover the pan and simmer for about 15 minutes or until the liquid has been absorbed. Set aside.
3 Heat the oil in a large pan, add the fish and fry for a few minutes, turning once. Remove with a slotted spoon and reserve. Add to the pan the onion, garlic and ginger and fry for

4–5 minutes, stirring frequently. Stir in the coriander, cumin and tomatoes and fry for 2–3 minutes. Add the water, cover and simmer for 10 minutes or until pulpy. Add the coconut milk and simmer until the mixture thickens. Add the reserved fish, spoon the sauce over the pieces and simmer for a further 5 minutes and then remove from the heat.

4 Grease a large ovenproof casserole and spread half the rice over the base. Spoon the fish mixture evenly over it and then top with the remaining rice. Cover and cook in an oven preheated to 325°F, 170°C, Gas Mark 3 for about 20 minutes. Remove and serve immediately.

Mussel and clam pilav

This, and similar recipes, are very popular in North America and there are many variations. This is one of my favourites.

Serve with a salad of your choice.

If you cannot find clams then use all mussels.

1 tablespoon fat or butter
3 rashers bacon, rind removed, cut into bite-sized pieces
1 large onion, chopped
1 clove garlic, crushed
1 large red or green pepper, seeded and chopped
225g (½lb) tomatoes, blanched, peeled and chopped
1 teaspoon salt
½ teaspoon black pepper
½ teaspoon chilli pepper
1 tablespoon brandy
450ml (¾ pint) stock
300ml (½ pint) dry white wine
20 mussels, scrubbed thoroughly
20 clams, scrubbed thoroughly

Pilav:
350g (12oz) long-grain rice, washed thoroughly under cold water and
  drained
600ml (1 pint) boiling water
120ml (4fl oz) dry white wine
1 teaspoon salt

Garnish:
2 tablespoons parsley

1 First prepare the pilav by placing all the ingredients in a large saucepan. Bring quickly to the boil, lower the heat, cover the pan and simmer for 15–20 minutes or until all the liquid has been absorbed. Turn off heat and set aside.

2 Melt the fat or butter in a saucepan and add the bacon. Fry until just crisp and then remove with a slotted spoon, drain on kitchen paper and reserve.

3 Add the onion and fry, stirring regularly, until soft. Add the garlic, red or green pepper and tomatoes and fry for a further 1–2 minutes. Stir in the salt, peppers, brandy and stock and bring to the boil. Lower the heat and simmer until the mixture thickens.

4 Meanwhile pour the wine into a large saucepan and add the mussels and clams. Cover the pan and steam over a medium heat just until the shells open. Remove the shellfish from the pan with a slotted spoon. Strain the wine and juices into the sauce and continue to simmer.

5 Pile the hot, cooked rice onto a large serving plate and arrange the shellfish over it. Pour the sauce over the top and sprinkle with the reserved bacon and the parsley.

Serve immediately.

Nasi goreng istimewa – shellfish and fried rice

A typical fried rice dish full of colour, texture and flavour from Indonesia. Serve the fried peanuts separately in small dishes.

Chopsticks –
'Laugh that you should be so busy to pick up morsels,
And put them into other mouths
With a life-time spent amid the sour and the bitter,
Can, or not, distinguish the flavours yourself?' – Yuan-mei,
1716–1758 *Penguin Book of Chinese Verse*

350g (12oz) long-grain rice, washed thoroughly under cold water and drained

600ml (1 pint) water
150ml (¼ pint) peanut or vegetable oil
450g (1lb) cooked chicken, cut into small pieces
225g (8oz) cooked pork, cut into thin, 1cm (½") pieces
175g (6oz) prawns or shrimps
2 large onions, chopped
2 cloves garlic, crushed
4 large chillis, coarsely chopped
1 tablespoon chopped coriander leaves
1 teaspoon cumin
½ teaspoon shrimp paste (Balachan) see Glossary
1 tablespoon brown sugar
2 bay leaves
2 teaspoons salt
225g (½lb) cooked crab or lobster meat, cut into small pieces

Omelette:
3 eggs
½ teaspoon salt
¼ teaspoon black pepper

Garnish:
110g (4oz) peanuts
3–4 spring onions, cut into 1cm (½") lengths

1 Place the rice in a saucepan with the water and bring to the
boil. Lower the heat, cover the pan and simmer until all the
liquid has been absorbed. Set aside.
2 Heat a little of the oil in a large pan or wok, add the chicken
and pork pieces and fry for 2–3 minutes, stirring regularly.
Remove with a slotted spoon and keep warm. Add a little more
oil to the pan, stir in the prawns or shrimps and fry for 2–3
minutes. Remove with a slotted spoon and keep warm.
3 Add a little more oil if needed and add half the onions, the
garlic, chilli peppers, coriander, cumin, shrimp paste, sugar,
bay leaves and salt. Fry for 5–6 minutes, stirring regularly.
Return the chicken, pork and shrimps to the pan and add the
crab or lobster. Cook over a low heat for a few minutes.
4 Fluff up the rice with a long-pronged fork and stir it
carefully into the onion mixture. Cover and leave over a very
low heat while you prepare the omelette.

5 Heat a little of the oil in a frying pan. Beat the eggs, salt and pepper together in a small bowl and pour half of it into the pan to make a thin omelette. Cook until pale golden on the under side. Turn it over, cook until the other side is just golden and slide onto a plate while you prepare the remaining egg mixture in the same way. Place the omelettes on top of each other, roll them up and then cut into thin strips. Keep warm.
6 Heat any remaining oil in the frying pan, add the rest of the chopped onion and fry until golden, stirring frequently. Remove with a slotted spoon and reserve. Drop the peanuts into the oil, fry for 2–3 minutes, remove and reserve.
7 To serve, transfer the rice mixture to a large serving dish. Garnish with the fried onion, omelette strips and spring onions. Serve the fried peanuts separately.

West Indian-style paella

The final recipe in this chapter, although from the West Indies, is in reality of Spanish inspiration with Indian overtones and Caribbean finish.

Like most paellas this is a filling meal. Serve it with khuri (page 220) and a fresh salad.

2 medium poussins or 1 small chicken, cut into serving pieces
225g (8oz) salt pork, cut into small cubes
2 medium onions, finely chopped
2 tart cooking apples, peeled, cored and diced
2 cloves garlic, crushed
½ teaspoon curry powder
1 tablespoon brown sugar
4 medium tomatoes, blanched, peeled and chopped
1 green or red pepper, seeded and chopped
350g (12oz) long-grain rice, washed under cold water and drained
450ml (¾ pint) water or stock
110g (4oz) raisins
50g (2oz) mixed nuts, chopped
350g (12oz) prawns or shrimps, peeled
120ml (4fl oz) dark rum

Garnish:
2 large plantains (see page 223)
2–3 tablespoons vegetable oil
75g (3oz) fresh pineapple chunks

Marinade:
1 clove garlic, crushed
2 tablespoons lemon juice
1 tablespoon soy sauce
1 teaspoon garam masala
1 level teaspoon chilli powder
1 level teaspoon salt
½ level teaspoon black pepper

1 Combine all the marinade ingredients in a large bowl. Add the chicken pieces and turn to coat thoroughly. Set aside for 1 hour. Remove chicken pieces and reserve the marinade.
2 Fry the salt pork in a large saucepan for 10 minutes, stirring regularly. Remove with a slotted spoon, drain on kitchen paper and reserve.
3 Add the chicken pieces to the pan and fry for about 10 minutes, turning regularly until evenly browned. Add a little oil if necessary. Remove with a slotted spoon and reserve.
4 Add the onions and fry until soft. Stir in the apples, garlic, curry powder, sugar, tomatoes and green or red pepper and fry for 4–5 minutes, stirring frequently. Stir in the rice and return the chicken pieces to the pan. Add the stock or water and boil vigorously for 1 minute. Lower the heat and stir in the raisins and mixed nuts. Cover and simmer for 15–20 minutes or until all the liquid has been absorbed.
5 Add the reserved marinade, salt pork, prawns or shrimps and the rum to the pilav and stir well. Re-cover the pan and cook over a low heat for a further 10 minutes.
6 Meanwhile fry the plantains as described in the recipe on page 223.
7 To serve turn the pilav into a large dish, arrange the pineapple chunks over the top and garnish with the fried plantains.

Burghul

Cracked Wheat

'Doon avar, chga tzavar.' – A house is a ruin without cracked wheat.
(Armenian saying)

Burghul is the Syrian (Arabic) name for cracked wheat. It is also known as Bourgouri (in Cyprus), Brighouri (Greece), Tzavar (Armenia) and Tzaouari (in Kurdistan).

Burghul is the staple diet of Armenians and, to a lesser extent of Syrians, Lebanese, Turks and Kurds. Outside this small geographical region of the Middle East it was until recently almost completely unknown.

Burghul consists of parboiled whole or crushed partially de-branned wheat grains. The biblical name for burghul was 'Arisah' – a name that has been retained in the ancient Middle Eastern dish 'Harissa' or Herisseh beloved of Armenians and Arabs (see page 157).

The age-old method of burghul preparation, which is still predominantly in use in village communities, is a very simple one. The wheat grains are boiled in a large cauldron until tender and then spread out in thin layers to dry in the sun. The outer bran layers are removed by sprinkling the cooked wheat with a little water and rubbing by hand. The grains are next cracked in a small round stone mill. These 'grinder mills' are depicted on Ancient Egyptian murals. They consist of two round stones, one on top of the other. The upper section has a small opening in the middle and space for a wooden handle. The sun-dried wheat is poured through the hole and the upper section of the grinder is turned round and round. The required size of the bulghur is controlled by gauging the space between the two stones. The grains are collected in large sheets of cloth which surround the grinder mill.

Today, of course, burghul is also produced in large manufacturing mills by a multi-stage process in which the moisture content is gradually increased by spraying with water and raising the temperature. When the moisture content has reached 40% the wheat is heated at 94°C (201°F) and then steamed for 15 minutes. The wheat is then cracked.

Burghul keeps well. It can be stored for up to 8 or 9 months under a wide range of temperature and humidity conditions. It is hard and brittle and thus discourages attacks by mites and insects.

The nutritive value of burghul is similar to that of the wheat from which it is made (see page 232).

Burghul in its three sizes is fast becoming popular in Europe and America. It can be purchased from most Continental and Indian shops as well as from some wholefood shops. Make sure you use the large grain burghul for all the pilav recipes in this section. The kibbeh recipes require fine grain burghul.

Tzavari pilav – cracked wheat pilav

This, the simplest of burghul pilavs is a family recipe; a favourite of my late father.

Serve it with any meat, fish, fowl or vegetable dish. In the villages of Anatolia the peasants pour fresh yoghurt over a plate of this pilav and consume it with gusto.

350g (12oz) large grain burghul
75g (3oz) butter
1 medium onion, finely chopped
600ml (1 pint) boiling water
1 teaspoon salt
½ teaspoon black pepper

1 Put the burghul into a bowl or fine sieve and wash under cold running water until the water runs clear. Leave to drain.
2 Melt the butter in a saucepan over a moderate heat. Add the onion and fry gently for 3–4 minutes or until soft and turning golden. Add the burghul and fry for 2–3 minutes, stirring constantly.
3 Stir in the boiling water, salt and pepper and boil vigorously for 1 minute. Lower the heat and simmer for about 15 minutes or until all the liquid has been absorbed. Turn off the heat, cover with a clean tea towel and leave to 'rest' for 10 minutes. Fluff up gently with a long-pronged fork and serve.

Variation: Telahaysov tzavari pilav – burghul pilav with vermicelli

Follow the directions above, but add 50g (2oz) vermicelli, broken into 2.5cm (1″) pieces, to the chopped onion and fry until the vermicelli is golden, stirring frequently.

Rehanov tzavari pilav – burghul pilav with basil

Cracked wheat, vermicelli, fresh basil and raisins are combined to create a delicious pilav which is excellent on its own with a bowl of fresh salad and some pickles, or as an accompaniment to meat and poultry dishes.

75g (3oz) butter
50g (2oz) vermicelli, broken into 2.5cm (1″) pieces
350g (12oz) large grain burghul, washed in a bowl or fine sieve until
  water runs clear
600ml (1 pint) boiling water
1 teaspoon salt
3 tablespoons raisins
5 tablespoons chopped fresh basil OR 2½ tablespoons dried basil
½ teaspoon black pepper

Garnish:
1 teaspoon paprika

1 Melt the butter in a saucepan, add the vermicelli and fry, stirring frequently until golden. Add the burghul and fry for a further 2–3 minutes, stirring constantly to coat with the butter.
2 Stir in the water, salt and raisins and boil vigorously for 1 minute. Lower the heat and simmer for 10 minutes. Carefully stir in the basil and black pepper and cook for a further 5–7 minutes or until all the liquid has been absorbed. Turn off the heat, cover with a clean tea towel and set aside to 'rest' for 10 minutes.
3 Fluff up with a long-pronged fork, spoon into a serving dish and sprinkle with the paprika.

Siserov tzavari pilav – burghul and chickpea pilav

Chickpeas and cracked wheat compliment each other well as this Lenten recipe testifies.

Although usually served warm with a bowl of yoghurt or as an accompaniment to meat dishes, it can also be served cold as a salad.

175g (6oz) chickpeas, soaked overnight in cold water
3 tablespoons oil
1 large onion, chopped
350g (12oz) large-grain burghul, washed in bowl or sieve until water
  runs clear
3 heaped tablespoons tomato purée
1 teaspoon salt
½ teaspoon black pepper
1 teaspoon paprika

Garnish:
2 tablespoons finely chopped parsley

1 Drain the chickpeas and remove their skins by squeezing each pea between thumb and forefinger. Place in a pan half-filled with water and bring to the boil. Lower the heat and simmer for 30–45 minutes or until tender, adding more boiling water if necessary. Drain the chickpeas and reserve the liquid.
2 Heat the oil in a large pan, add the onion and fry until soft and golden. Add the chickpeas and burghul and fry for 1 minute. Stir in the tomato purée, salt, black pepper and paprika. If necessary make the reserved liquid up to 600ml (1 pint) with boiling water and add to the pan. Boil vigorously for 1 minute and then lower the heat and simmer until all the liquid has been absorbed.
3 Turn off the heat, cover the pan with a clean tea towel and leave to 'rest' for 10 minutes. Fluff up with a long-pronged fork, spoon into a serving dish and sprinkle with the parsley.

Loligov tzavari pilav – tomato and burghul pilav

In this pilav, burghul's earthy taste is enhanced by another flavour – that of curry powder.

75g (3oz) butter
1 large onion, finely chopped
2 tablespoons blanched almonds
225g (8oz) tomatoes, blanched, peeled and chopped
1 teaspoon curry powder
350g (12oz) large-grain burghul, washed in a bowl or sieve until the
  water runs clear
1 teaspoon salt
½ teaspoon black pepper
600ml (1 pint) boiling water or stock

1 Melt the butter in a pan, add the onion and fry until soft and
turning golden. Add the almonds and fry, stirring constantly,
until they are evenly golden.
2 Stir in the tomatoes and curry powder and fry for 2–3
minutes. Add the burghul and turn to coat with the mixture.
Add the remaining ingredients and bring to the boil. Boil
vigorously for 1 minute and then lower the heat and simmer
for about 15 minutes or until all the liquid has been absorbed.
3 Turn off the heat, cover with a clean tea towel and leave to
'rest' for 10 minutes. Fluff up with a long-pronged fork and
serve.

Tahinov tzavari yeghintz – burghul pilav with tahina sauce

Chickpeas, red and green pepper and diced carrots are added to
the cracked wheat and the whole is then topped with a sauce of
tahina and garlic. The result is a colourful and tasty pilav
which is excellent served with a bowl of salad, olives and
pickles.

75g (3oz) chickpeas, soaked overnight in cold water
4 tablespoons oil
1 red pepper, seeded and diced
1 green pepper, seeded and diced
3 carrots, peeled and diced
350g (12oz) large-grain burghul, washed in a bowl or sieve until water
  runs clear
1 teaspoon salt
1 teaspoon cumin
½ teaspoon chilli pepper

Sauce:
2 cloves garlic, crushed
150ml (¼ pint) water
150ml (¼ pint) tahina – see Glossary

Garnish:
2 tablespoons chopped parsley

1 Drain the chickpeas and remove the skins by squeezing each pea between thumb and forefinger. Place in a saucepan half-filled with water and bring to the boil. Lower the heat and simmer for 30–45 minutes or until tender, adding more boiling water if necessary. Drain and reserve the liquid.
2 Heat the oil in a large saucepan, add the vegetables and fry for 4–5 minutes to soften. Stir in the chickpeas and all the remaining ingredients. Make the reserved liquid up to 600ml (1 pint) and add to the pan. Bring to the boil and boil vigorously for 1 minute. Lower the heat and simmer for about 15 minutes or until all the liquid has been absorbed.
3 Remove from the heat, cover with a clean tea towel and set aside while you prepare the sauce. Mix the garlic and water together in a small bowl. Slowly pour the tahina into the bowl, stirring constantly. The consistency should be that of thick cream. If it is too thick stir in a little more water.
4 Fluff up the burghul with a long-pronged fork and spoon into a shallow dish. Either pour the sauce over the top or serve in a sauceboat. Sprinkle with the parsley and serve.

Kirmizi fasulyali bourgoul pilavi – burghul and red kidney bean pilav

A fine dish from Central Anatolia.

175g (6oz) red kidney beans, soaked in cold water overnight
75g (3oz) butter
1 large onion, thinly sliced
3 medium carrots, peeled and cut into thin rings
¼ white cabbage, thinly sliced
350g (12oz) large-grain burghul, washed in a bowl or sieve until water
  runs clear

2 tablespoons blanched almonds
600ml (1 pint) water, boiling
1 teaspoon dillweed
1 teaspoon salt
2 tablespoons pomegranate juice – see page 227

1 Drain the beans and place in a saucepan half-filled with
water. Bring to the boil, cook vigorously for 10 minutes then
lower the heat and simmer for 45–60 minutes or until the
beans are tender. Add more boiling water if necessary. Drain
and reserve.
2 Melt the butter in a large pan, add the onion and fry until
soft. Add the carrots and cabbage and fry for 3–4 minutes,
stirring frequently. Add the burghul and almonds and fry for a
further 2–3 minutes. Return the beans to the pan and stir in
the remaining ingredients. Boil vigorously for 1 minute, then
lower the heat and simmer for about 15 minutes or until all the
liquid has been absorbed.
3 Turn off the heat, cover with a clean tea towel and leave to
'rest' for 10 minutes. Fluff up with a long-pronged fork, turn
into a large dish and serve with yoghurt and salad.

Burghul-bi-spanikh – burghul and spinach pilav

'The wheat turns round and round and comes back to the hole in the
mill.' – i.e. home is best *(Arab saying)*

A popular Syrian–Lebanese dish.
    Spinach and cracked wheat are most compatible. Pine
kernels are rather expensive – though very cheap in Lebanon!
– so I suggest you use almonds or walnuts instead. Serve with
yoghurt, salad and some pickles of your choice.

90ml (3fl oz) oil
1 large onion, finely chopped
2 cloves garlic, finely chopped
3 tablespoons pine kernels or chopped walnuts
450g (1lb) spinach, coarse leaves and stems discarded, washed
  thoroughly and coarsely chopped

350g (12oz) large-grain burghul, washed in bowl or sieve until water
  runs clear
1 teaspoon salt
½ teaspoon black pepper
1 teaspoon dillweed
600ml (1 pint) boiling water or stock

1 Heat the oil in a saucepan, add the onion and fry until soft
and turning golden. Add the garlic and fry for a further 1–2
minutes. Stir in the nuts and spinach, cover the pan and cook
for 3–4 minutes or until the spinach is slightly limp.
2 Stir in the remaining ingredients and boil vigorously for
1 minute. Lower the heat and simmer for about 15 minutes or
until the liquid has been absorbed.
3 Turn off the heat, cover with a clean tea towel and leave to
'rest' for 10 minutes before serving.

Soongov tzavari pilav – burghul and mushroom pilav

Onions, mushrooms and fenugreek give this dish a very
distinctive flavour and character.
  Ideal with grilled meat and fish.

75g (3oz) butter
6 spring onions, thinly sliced
2 cloves garlic, crushed
225g (8oz) button mushrooms, wiped clean and halved
1 green pepper, seeded and thinly sliced
350g (12oz) large-grain burghul, washed in bowl or sieve until water
  runs clean
1 level teaspoon ground fenugreek
1 teaspoon brown sugar
1 teaspoon salt
600ml (1 pint) boiling water or stock

Garnish:
2 tablespoons slivered almonds

1 Melt the butter in a saucepan, add the onions and garlic and
fry for 2–3 minutes. Stir in the mushrooms and green pepper
and fry for a further 2–3 minutes to soften. Add the burghul

and stir well to coat with the butter. Stir in the remaining ingredients and boil vigorously for 1 minute. Lower the heat and simmer for about 15 minutes or until all the liquid has been absorbed.

2 Turn off the heat, cover with a clean tea towel and leave to 'rest' for 10 minutes. Meanwhile toast the almonds until golden.

3 To serve fluff up the pilav with a long-pronged fork, spoon into a large dish and sprinkle with the almonds.

Mujaddarah – burghul and lentil pilav

This is a dish of ancient origins. Rice and lentil dishes appear throughout the Middle East and India, under different names and often with other vegetables. The most famed Arab dish is 'Muddara' (p. 28) where rice is used. The recipe below, using cracked wheat, is beloved of Syrians, Armenians and Anatolian Turks.

Serve on its own with a bowl of salad, yoghurt and pickles.

225g (8oz) green or continental lentils, washed and drained
300ml (½ pint) olive or vegetable oil
3 large onions, thinly sliced
1½ teaspoons salt
¾ teaspoon black pepper
225g (8oz) large-grain burghul, washed in a bowl or sieve until water
  runs clear

1 Place the lentils in a saucepan half-filled with water and bring to the boil. Lower the heat and simmer for about 20 minutes or until the lentils are only just tender. Drain the lentils and reserve the liquid.

2 Meanwhile heat the oil in a large frying pan, add the onions and fry, stirring frequently, until dark golden, but not burnt. Transfer half the fried onion, with a slotted spoon, to a large saucepan and reserve the remaining onion with its oil.

3 Add the lentils to the onions in the large pan and stir in the salt and pepper. Pour 600ml (1 pint) of the reserved liquid – make up with water if insufficient – into the pan and bring to the boil. Stir in the burghul, lower the heat and simmer for

about 15 minutes or until the liquid has been absorbed.
Remove from the heat, cover with a clean tea towel and leave
to 'rest' for 10 minutes.
4 Pile the pilav onto a large plate and garnish with the
remaining onion and oil.

Burghul-bi-kamah – burghul and truffle pilav

A speciality of the Aleppo region in Syria.

450g (1lb) truffles, soaked in warm water for 30 minutes
75g (3oz) butter
1 large onion, thinly sliced
2 tablespoons pine kernels or slivered almonds
1 teaspoon salt
½ teaspoon chilli pepper
1 teaspoon paprika
600ml (1 pint) boiling water
350g (12oz) large-grain burghul, washed in bowl or sieve until water
  runs clean
2 bay leaves

1 Drain the truffles and scrub under running water. Peel each
one carefully with the point of a sharp knife, rinsing out any
earthy deposits in the holes and folds. Cut into thin strips.
2 Melt the butter in a saucepan, add the onion and fry for a
few minutes until soft. Add the pine kernels or almonds and fry
for 2 minutes, stirring constantly. Stir in the prepared truffles,
salt, chilli pepper, paprika and half the water. Cover and
simmer for 20 minutes.
3 Add the burghul, bay leaves and remaining water and stir
well. Boil vigorously for 1 minute, lower the heat and simmer
for about 15 minutes or until all the liquid has been absorbed.
4 Turn off the heat, cover with a clean tea towel and leave to
'rest' for 10 minutes before fluffing up with a long-pronged fork
and serving.

Tzaouri-bi-tamar – burghul and date pilav

This is a recipe from the Kurdish regions of Iraq where cracked
wheat is still predominant, while in the rest of the country rice
is all prevailing.

The date, of course, is one of the glories of Iraqi horticulture.
The land is literally palmed with the tree so beloved of the
Bedouin, Omar Khayyam and his ilk – not forgetting the
Prophet himself.

In other regions of the Middle East this recipe is prepared
with rice.

Ideal with roast and grilled lamb.

75g (3oz) butter
75g (3oz) hazelnuts, coarsely chopped
350g (12oz) large-grain burghul, washed in bowl or sieve until water
  runs clear
1 teaspoon salt
600ml (1 pint) boiling water

Garnish:
50g (2oz) butter
110g (4oz) stoned dates, chopped
50g (2oz) raisins or sultanas

1 Melt the butter in a saucepan, add the nuts and fry for 1–2
minutes, stirring constantly. Stir in the burghul and fry for a
further 2–3 minutes. Add the salt and water and boil
vigorously for 1 minute. Lower the heat and simmer for about
15 minutes or until all the liquid has been absorbed. Turn off
the heat, cover with a clean tea towel and leave to 'rest' for 10
minutes.
2 Meanwhile prepare the garnish by melting the butter in a
large frying pan. Add the fruit and fry for 3–4 minutes,
stirring regularly.
3 To serve spoon the pilav into a large dish and arrange the
fruit mixture over the top.

Chirov tzavari pilav – burghul with fruit and nuts

'He went to Yerevan to buy rice, and returned to find his tzavar
stolen.' – *Armenian saying*

Makes a marvellous savoury dish. Ideal for a buffet.

75g (3oz) butter
350g (12oz) large-grain burghul, washed in a bowl or sieve until water
   runs clear
1 teaspoon salt
50g (2oz) raisins or sultanas
75g (3oz) dried apricots, soaked overnight, drained and thinly sliced
75g (3oz) prunes, soaked overnight, drained and thinly sliced
600ml (1 pint) boiling water

Garnish:
50g (2oz) butter
50g (2oz) hazelnuts, coarsely chopped
50g (2oz) pine kernels
25g (1oz) blanched almonds

1 Melt the butter in a large saucepan, add the burghul and fry
for 2–3 minutes, stirring frequently. Stir in the remaining
ingredients and boil vigorously for 1 minute. Lower the heat
and simmer for about 15 minutes or until all the liquid has
been absorbed. Remove from the heat, cover with a clean tea
towel and leave to 'rest' for 10 minutes.
2 Meanwhile prepare the garnish by melting the butter in a
frying pan. Add the nuts and fry, stirring frequently, for a few
minutes until they begin to turn golden. Remove with a slotted
spoon.
3 To serve fluff up the pilav with a long-pronged fork, turn it
into a large dish and sprinkle the fried nuts over the top.

Gigerov tzavari pilav – liver and burghul pilav

A filling meal. Serve with a fresh salad.

110g (4oz) chickpeas, soaked overnight in cold water
110g (4oz) butter
350g (12oz) calf's or lamb's liver, coarsely chopped

1 teaspoon salt
¼ teaspoon black pepper
1 large onion, thinly sliced
2 large tomatoes, blanched, peeled and chopped
2 sticks celery, thinly sliced
225g (8oz) large-grain burghul, washed in bowl or sieve until water
  runs clear
2 tablespoons chopped parsley
450ml (¾ pint) boiling water

1 Drain the chickpeas and remove their skins by squeezing
each pea between thumb and forefinger. Place in a saucepan
half-filled with water and bring to the boil. Lower the heat and
simmer for 30–45 minutes or until tender. Add more boiling
water if necessary. Drain and reserve.
2 Melt half the butter in a saucepan, add the chopped liver and
fry for 2–3 minutes, stirring regularly. Season with the salt
and pepper and set aside.
3 Melt the remaining butter in another pan, add the onion and
fry until soft and turning golden. Add the tomatoes and celery
and cook for a further 2–3 minutes. Stir in the burghul,
parsley, reserved chickpeas, liver and water. Boil vigorously
for 1 minute, lower the heat and simmer for about 15 minutes
or until all the liquid has been absorbed.
4 Remove from the heat, cover with a tea towel and leave to
'rest' for 10 minutes. Fluff up with a long-pronged fork and
serve.

Kinedan pilav – wine-bar pilav

My late father's personal favourite, and a top favourite of
people from the cities of Kilis and Antab in Southern Turkey.
   This pilav was served in the Middle Eastern bars as an
accompaniment to raki or some of the strong local wines, hence
the name.
   It is wholesome and very tasty and my father, for one, could
never have enough of it.

3 tablespoons oil
1 large onion, chopped

1kg (2lb) minced lamb or beef
2 green peppers, seeded and chopped
675g (1½lb) tomatoes, blanched, peeled and coarsely chopped
2 tablespoons tomato purée
1½ teaspoons salt
¾ teaspoon black pepper
900ml (1½ pints) boiling water
350g (12oz) large-grain burghul, washed in bowl or sieve until water
   runs clear

1 Heat the oil in a large saucepan, add the onion and fry for a
few minutes until soft. Add the meat and fry for about
10 minutes until browned, stirring regularly and breaking up
the lumps with a wooden spoon.
2 Stir in the peppers and tomatoes and cook for a further
5 minutes.
3 Add the tomato purée, salt, pepper and 300ml (½ pint) of the
water. Mix well and simmer over a moderate heat until the
water has evaporated and the mixture is dry.
4 Mix in the burghul and remaining water and boil vigorously
for 1 minute. Lower the heat and simmer until all the liquid
has been absorbed. Remove from the heat, cover with a clean
tea towel and leave to 'rest' for a few minutes before serving.

   Serve with some pickles, salad and/or yoghurt and perhaps a
glass of raki (also known as arak, oghi and ouzo)!

Tzavarov garidosi pilav – burghul and shrimp pilav

A delicious pilav from the shores of the Black Sea, which is
famed for her shrimps, sardines, whitebait and, above all for
'Hamsi' (anchovies).
   Serve with a salad of your choice.

25g (1oz) butter
60ml (2fl oz) oil
675g (1½lb) shrimps
1 teaspoon salt
1 teaspoon cumin
1 large onion, thinly sliced
2 cloves garlic, crushed

225g (8oz) tomatoes, blanched, peeled and chopped
3 sticks celery, thinly sliced
2 tablespoons chopped parsley or mint
350g (12oz) large-grain burghul, washed in bowl or sieve until water
  runs clear
600ml (1 pint) boiling water

1 Heat the butter and oil in a large pan. Add the shrimps, salt
and cumin and fry for 2–3 minutes, turning carefully and
regularly. Remove the shrimps with a slotted spoon and
reserve.
2 Add the onion and garlic and fry until soft and turning
brown. Stir in the tomatoes, celery and parsley or mint and
cook for 3–4 minutes. Stir in the burghul and water and boil
for 1 minute. Lower the heat and simmer for 5 minutes.
3 Arrange the reserved shrimps on top of the burghul, cover
the pan and simmer for a further 10–15 minutes or until all
the liquid has been absorbed.
4 Turn off the heat, cover with a tea towel and leave to 'rest'
for 10 minutes. Carefully fluff up with a long-pronged fork and
serve.

Beyinli bourgoul pilavi – burghul and brain pilav

An Anatolian dish of supreme refinement.
  It makes an excellent savoury with a bowl of salad and
yoghurt.

450g (1lb) lamb's or calf's brains
2 tablespoons vinegar
1 tablespoon salt
75g (3oz) butter
50g (2oz) vermicelli, broken into 2.5cm (1") pieces
350g (12oz) large-grain burghul, washed in a bowl or sieve until water
  runs clear
2 teaspoons dillweed
1 teaspoon salt
½ teaspoon black pepper
1 teaspoon paprika
600ml (1 pint) boiling water

1 Place the brains in a large bowl, add half the vinegar and salt and enough cold water to cover and leave to soak for at least 1 hour, changing the water 2–3 times.

2 Remove the brains, rinse and cut away and discard the loose outer membranes.

3 Place the brains in a saucepan, add enough water to cover and the remaining vinegar. Bring to the boil. Lower the heat and simmer for 5 minutes. Drain. When cool enough to handle cut them into 2cm (¾") pieces and reserve.

4 Melt the butter in a saucepan, add the vermicelli and fry until golden, stirring frequently. Stir in the burghul and fry for another minute or two. Add the dillweed, salt, pepper, paprika and water and boil for 1 minute. Lower the heat, stir in the brains and simmer for about 15 minutes or until all the liquid has been absorbed.

5 Turn off the heat, cover with a tea towel and leave to 'rest' for 10 minutes before serving.

Piliç bourgoul pilavi – burghul pilav with poussin

A very popular dish from Turkey. Traditionally small chicken, poussin or even pigeons were used for this dish, but there is no reason why you cannot use half a chicken instead. In Syria and Iraq small birds such as thrush, quail, woodcock etc. are used.

Serve with a fresh salad and some pickles.

2 poussin OR ½ chicken
50g (2oz) butter or ghee
1 large onion, chopped
25g (1oz) vermicelli, broken into 2.5cm (1") pieces
3 green chilli peppers, seeded and thinly sliced
350g (12oz) large-grain burghul, washed in bowl or sieve until water
  runs clear
600ml (1 pint) chicken stock
2 tablespoons sultanas
1 teaspoon salt
½ teaspoon allspice
2 cloves

1 Place the poussin or chicken half in a large saucepan, cover

with water and bring to the boil. Lower the heat and simmer
for 30–45 minutes or until tender. Remove the poussin or
chicken and set aside to cool. Reserve the stock.

2 When the poussin are cool enough to handle cut each one
into 8 pieces – 2 breasts, 2 wings, 2 drumsticks and 2 thighs.
Remove the skin from each piece. If using half a chicken,
discard the skin and bones and cut the flesh into bite-sized
pieces.

3 Melt the butter or ghee in a large saucepan, add the chicken
pieces and fry until evenly golden. Remove with a slotted spoon
and reserve. Add the onion and vermicelli and fry until the
onion is soft and the vermicelli golden. Add the burghul and
fry for 1–2 minutes, stirring frequently. Return the chicken
pieces to the pan and stir in all the remaining ingredients.
Bring to the boil, lower the heat and simmer until all the liquid
has been absorbed.

4 Turn off the heat, cover with a tea towel and leave to 'rest'
for 10 minutes before serving.

Burghul bidfeen – lamb and burghul pilav with sesame seeds

An Arab favourite. Lamb is the traditional meat, but beef, and
even goat, can be substituted.

   Serve with a bowl of salad and some yoghurt.

50g (2oz) butter or ghee
450g (1lb) lean leg or shoulder of lamb, cut into thin strips about
   2.5cm (1″) long
1 teaspoon salt
½ teaspoon black pepper
½ teaspoon chilli pepper
1 teaspoon cumin
350g (12oz) large-grain burghul, washed in bowl or sieve until water
   runs clear
600ml (1 pint) boiling water
75g (3oz) sesame seeds

1 Melt the butter or ghee in a large saucepan, add the meat,
salt, black pepper, chilli pepper and cumin and fry for 5–10
minutes, stirring frequently.

2 Stir in the burghul and water and boil vigorously for
1 minute. Lower the heat and simmer for about 15 minutes or
until all the liquid has been absorbed.
3 Meanwhile spread the sesame seeds out on kitchen foil and
toast under the grill until golden, stirring regularly. Reserve.
4 When the pilav is cooked fluff it up with a long-pronged fork
and stir in the toasted sesame seeds. Cover and leave to rest for
a few minutes and then serve.

Kibbeh

'Kibbeh' or 'kibbi' is the colloquial Syrian Arabic for
'kubaybah' which means 'to form a ball'. The basic ingredients
for kibbeh are burghul and meat. From these two simple
ingredients many tasty dishes are prepared, some served as
hors d'oeuvre and some as entrées.

Lamb is the traditional meat used, but you can substitute
lean beef. Kibbeh can be eaten raw, boiled, grilled, fried or
baked. To prevent its falling apart during the cooking process
the general rule is to use the meat and burghul in approximate
proportions of 1½:½.

For kibbeh dishes always use small-grain burghul.

The first recipe is from Lebanon. It appears on every
restaurant table and in every house and is always
accompanied by Cos lettuce, onion slices and, naturally, a glass
or two of arak.

Kibbeh naya – Lebanese raw meat with burghul

This dish is served as an hors d'oeuvre or as a savoury.

75g (3oz) fine burghul
1 teaspoon salt
½ teaspoon black pepper
175g (6oz) very lean lamb or beef, minced twice
1½ tablespoons very finely chopped onion
1½ tablespoons olive oil
½ teaspoon chilli pepper
2 tablespoons pine kernels

Accompaniments:
2 onions, quartered
Cos lettuce leaves

1 Wash the burghul in a bowl until the water poured off is
clear. Drain and turn onto a baking sheet. Season with the salt
and black pepper and knead for 5 minutes, wetting your hands
if the mixture sticks to them. Add the minced meat and
chopped onion and knead for a further 5–10 minutes until the
mixture is smooth. Keep wetting your hands to make the
kneading easier.
2 .To serve spread the kibbeh mixture over a large plate and
press until smooth, forming a slight depression in the middle.
Pour the olive oil into the centre and sprinkle the chilli pepper
all over the surface. Scatter the pine kernels over the top and
serve immediately accompanied by the onion and lettuce.

Variation: – Kibbeh naya-bi-mohammasa raw kibbeh with meat sauce

Mohammasa is a meat and nut sauce that often accompanies
the raw kibbeh. It is served in a separate dish and is more
liquid than the meat sauce which accompanies the kibbeh in
the recipe for 'Houm Miss' following this recipe.

Kibbeh:
See above

Meat sauce:
25g (1oz) butter
50g (2oz) onion, very finely chopped
110g (4oz) minced meat
2 tablespoons lemon juice
½ teaspoon salt
¼ teaspoon cinnamon
¼ teaspoon chilli pepper
150ml (¼ pint) boiling water
1 tablespoon pine kernels

1 Melt the butter in a small pan, add the onion and fry until
soft. Add the meat and fry for about 5 minutes, stirring

regularly. Stir in all the remaining ingredients and simmer over a low-moderate heat for 10–15 minutes or until the meat is cooked.

2 Turn into a small bowl and serve with the kibbeh.

Houm miss – Armenian-style raw meat with burghul

In this version the kibbeh mixture is shaped into 'patties', dipped into the meat mixture and then eaten.

It is a wholesome and attractive dish and is best made just before you are ready to eat it as it will dry fairly quickly.

175g (6oz) fine burghul
175g (6oz) very lean lamb, minced twice
1 tablespoon onion, very finely chopped
1 teaspoon salt
½ teaspoon black pepper
½ teaspoon chilli pepper

Meat sauce:
110g (4oz) minced lamb
1 tablespoon chopped onion
50g (2oz) chopped walnuts
½ teaspoon salt
¼ teaspoon black pepper
1 tablespoon parsley, finely chopped

Garnish:
pine kernels or split almonds
1 tablespoon parsley, chopped

1 First prepare the meat sauce by placing the meat and onion in a small pan and frying, over a low heat, for 10–15 minutes, stirring frequently. Add the walnuts, salt and pepper and continue to fry until the meat is cooked. Stir in the parsley and set aside.

2 Wash the burghul in a bowl until the water poured off is clear. Drain and turn onto a baking sheet. Knead for 5 minutes, dampening your hands with warm water occasionally. Add the lean lamb, onion, salt, black and chilli

peppers and knead for 5–10 minutes, dampening your hands
occasionally.
3 Wet your hands, take a walnut-sized piece of the kibbeh
mixture and squeeze it in the palm of your hand to make a boat
shape. Use up all the mixture in this way and arrange the
patties around the edge of a large serving plate.
4 Stick one pine kernel or split almond into the top of each
piece. Heat the cooked meat through thoroughly, spoon it
into the middle of the plate and sprinkle with the parsley.

Amram – grilled kibbeh

The kibbeh mixture can be grilled over charcoal or under the
grill with great success.

   A basic kibbeh recipe can be used with equal success for
frying and boiling. The recipe below is a standard one and you
can use it wherever possible. Recipes that are different will be
given in full.

250g (9oz) fine burghul, washed in bowl or sieve until water is clear
350g (¾lb) lean lamb, minced twice
2 tablespoons very finely chopped onion
1½ teaspoons salt
¾ teaspoon black pepper
½ teaspoon chilli pepper
1½ teaspoons allspice

1 Spread the burghul out on a baking sheet and set aside
while you prepare the meat.
2 Place the meat in a bowl, add the onion, seasonings and
2 tablespoons of water and knead until well blended and
smooth. Add this to the burghul and knead until all the
burghul is gathered up with the meat into a ball. Keeping your
hands damp, knead the mixture for at least 10 minutes. Do not
skimp on the kneading time or the kibbeh will be coarse when
cooked.
3 Divide the mixture into 18 even portions. Roll each into a
ball and then flatten into a round 7–10cm (3–4″) in diameter
and about 1cm (½″) thick.

4 Cook over charcoal or under the grill for about 10 minutes, turning occasionally.
5 Serve on a bed of lettuce leaves with a bowl of yoghurt as an accompaniment.

Variation: Kibbeh mishwiyeh – skewered kibbeh

1 Prepare the kibbeh mixture as described in the recipe above.
2 Divide the mixture into 18–24 small balls. Slide a skewer through each and, with lightly dampened palms, gently squeeze the kibbeh out to form a thin sausage.
3 Cook over charcoal for about 8–10 minutes, turning occasionally.
4 Serve immediately with fresh salad, yoghurt and some pickles.

Vospov kufta – lentil kibbeh

'Kufta' derives from old Aramaic (the language in which Jesus spoke) and means minced or shredded, hence 'kufta kebab' or 'kofta kobob'.

Kufta dishes are not only made with minced meat, but often include rice, burghul, lentils, chickpeas etc. In this 'classic' dish lentils replace meat, making an ideal vegetarian dish – and that was its original function as Vospov Kufta is a Lenten meal of the Orthodox Christian churches of Armenia and Lebanon. Serve it with a fresh salad, yoghurt and pickles.

225g (8oz) green or continental lentils, rinsed and drained
1.2l (2 pints) water
2 teaspoons salt
175g (6oz) fine burghul, washed in a bowl or sieve until water runs clear
240ml (8fl oz) olive oil
1 large onion, finely chopped
3 spring onions, including green tops, finely chopped
3 tablespoons finely chopped parsley
3 tablespoons finely chopped fresh mint OR 1½ tablespoons dried mint

Garnish:
Paprika

1 Put the lentils in a large saucepan with the water and salt.
Bring to the boil and simmer for about 30 minutes or until the
lentils are tender. Add a little more water if necessary.
2 Stir in the burghul and half the oil. Simmer for a few
minutes and then turn off the heat, cover and set aside for 15
minutes. At the end of this time all the liquid should have been
absorbed.
3 Meanwhile heat the remaining oil in a small pan, add the
chopped onion and fry until soft and golden.
4 Empty the lentil–burghul mixture into a large bowl and add
the fried onion with its oil. Knead the mixture well, keeping
your hands damp with warm water, until smooth. Mix in half
the spring onions, green pepper, parsley and mint. Taste and
adjust seasoning if necessary.
5 Keeping your hands moist, shape the mixture into small
patties about 2.5–4cm (1″–1½″) long and 2cm (¾″) wide.
Arrange on a serving dish and sprinkle with the paprika and
remaining spring onion, green pepper, parsley and mint. Serve
warm.

Fillings for kibbeh

Kibbeh fries beautifully and the basic kibbeh mixture (see
Amram, page 131) can be shaped into walnut-sized balls and
fried in butter or oil. However, by far the most popular fried
kibbehs are those which have fillings of meat, suet, vegetables,
eggs, etc. The first three fillings below are standard ones for
kibbeh tarablousieh. After that there are a further two
variations, one with boiled eggs and the other with spinach
and nuts.

Meat and onion filling:

2 tablespoons oil or ghee
225g (8oz) minced meat
2 onions, finely chopped

1 teaspoon salt
25g (1oz) pine kernels or chopped walnuts
½ teaspoon black pepper
½ teaspoon allspice
½ teaspoon cinnamon
1 tablespoon dried rose petals (optional)

1 Heat the oil or ghee in a saucepan, add the meat and fry for
5 minutes, stirring frequently. Add the onions and salt and fry
for 30 minutes until the meat is cooked. Add the remaining
ingredients, mix well and set aside to cool.
2 You can prepare this filling well in advance, cover and
refrigerate. It can be used for any stuffed kibbeh including
kibbeh-bil-sanieh.

Suet filling:

225g (8oz) lamb or beef suet
25g (1oz) chopped walnuts or pine kernels
½ teaspoon black pepper
½ teaspoon allspice
1 teaspoon salt

1 Either blend all the ingredients in a mixer or knead them
together thoroughly.
2 Chill for several hours before handling.

Butter or margarine filling:

Follow the recipe for suet filling above, but use 225g (8oz) block
butter or margarine instead of the suet.

Kibbeh tarablousieh – fried Tripoli-style kibbeh

These kibbeh are usually oval-shaped, filled with a meat
mixture and fried. They can be made in a variety of sizes from
those the size of bird's eggs to others as much as 7.5cm (3″) in
length. The smaller versions are usually served as hors
d'oeuvre, while the larger ones are eaten as a main meal.

Makes about 20 medium-sized kibbeh.

Filling:
See meat and onion filling above.

Kibbeh:
225g (8oz) fine burghul, washed in bowl or sieve until water runs
  clear, then drained
450g (1lb) lean lamb, minced twice
2 tablespoons onion, very finely chopped
2 teaspoons salt
1 teaspoon black pepper

To cook:
oil for deep-frying

To serve:
lemon wedges

1 First prepare the filling as described in the relevant recipe
and set it aside.
2 Spread the burghul out on a baking sheet and knead for a
few minutes. Add the meat, onion and seasonings and knead
for about 10 minutes, keeping your hands damp with warm
water.
3 To stuff the kibbeh, wet your hands and break off an
egg-sized piece of kibbeh. Hold this ball of kibbeh in the palm
of one hand and, with the index finger of the other hand, make
a hole in the kibbeh. Press the index finger down into the palm
of the other hand squeezing out the kibbeh and making the
shell a little thinner. Slowly rotate the ball of kibbeh so that
the finger is pressing down on a new part of the kibbeh shell
and making it thinner. Continue turning the shell round and
round and pressing it up the finger until you have a long oval
shape with a slightly wider mouth. The art is to get the shell as
thin as possible without cracking it. It is easier to do this if you
keep your hands damp.
4 Place a heaped teaspoon of the filling into the shell and then
close the opening by drawing the edges together and sealing.
Wet your hands again and roll the kibbeh between your palms
to smooth off and ensure that it is a real oval shape. Continue
in this way until you have used up all the kibbeh mixture and
filling.

5 To cook, heat sufficient oil to deep-fry. Add a few kibbeh at a
time and fry for 10–15 minutes, turning occasionally, until
golden. Remove and drain. Keep warm while you cook the rest
in the same way.

Serve hot with the lemon wedges. To eat cut the kibbeh in
half and squeeze lemon juice over the filling.

NB These kibbeh will freeze very successfully, but thaw
them thoroughly before frying.

Variations:

a) Kibbeh-bi-halabieh – kibbeh with boiled egg filling

1 Follow the recipe above but substitute the meat filling with
small whole eggs. Boil the requisite number of eggs for 1
minute then cool and shell.
2 Mould the kibbeh around the egg and fry as described above.
3 Serve with lemon wedges, olives, salads and pickles.

b) Dabgvadz kufta-shominov – kibbeh with spinach stuffing

Filling:
450g (1lb) fresh spinach, coarse stems and leaves discarded
4 tablespoons oil
1 large onion, chopped
50g (2oz) chopped walnuts
50g (2oz) raisins
1 teaspoon salt
½ teaspoon black pepper
½ teaspoon allspice

Kibbeh:
See recipe for Kibbeh tarablousieh above.

1 To prepare the filling wash the spinach thoroughly to get rid
of all sand and dirt. Half fill a pan with lightly salted water
and bring to the boil. Add the spinach and simmer for 5
minutes. Drain into a colander and, when cool enough to
handle squeeze out as much liquid as possible and chop finely.

2 Heat the oil in a pan, add the onion and fry until soft and golden. Add the spinach, nuts, raisins and seasonings and fry for 4–5 minutes, stirring frequently. Set aside to cool.

3 Prepare the kibbeh as described above and fill with the spinach mixture.

Kibbeh-bil sanieh – kibbeh baked in a tray

This is a classic Syrian dish.
  Serve with yoghurt, salad and pickles.

Filling:
3 tablespoons oil
50g (2oz) pine kernels or chopped walnuts
350g (12oz) minced meat
1 large onion, chopped
1 teaspoon salt
1 level teaspoon black pepper
1 level teaspoon allspice
½ teaspoon cinnamon
2 tablespoons finely chopped parsley

Kibbeh:
250g (9oz) fine burghul, washed in bowl or sieve until water runs
  clear, then drained
350g (12oz) lean lamb or beef, minced twice
2 tablespoons very finely chopped onion
1½ teaspoons salt
1 teaspoon black pepper

To cook:
Pinch allspice
75g (3oz) butter
3 tablespoons oil mixed with 6 tablespoons water

1 First prepare the filling by heating the oil in a saucepan. Add the nuts, fry for 2–3 minutes and then remove with a slotted spoon, drain and reserve. Add the meat to the pan and fry for 15 minutes, stirring frequently to break up any lumps. Add the onion, seasonings and spices and cook for a further 20–30 minutes, stirring frequently. Stir in the nuts and parsley and set aside.

2 Spread the burghul out on a baking tray and knead for a few minutes. Add the lamb, onion and seasonings and knead for at least 10 minutes, keeping your hands damp with warm water. Divide the mixture into 2 equal parts.

3 Butter a shallow baking dish at least 2.5cm (1″) deep and about 30cm (12″) in diameter OR 30 × 25cm (12″ × 10″) and sprinkle the base with a little allspice. With your fingers spread one half of the kibbeh mixture evenly over the bottom of the dish. Spread the filling evenly over it. Arrange the remaining kibbeh evenly over the top. The easiest way of doing this is to break off lumps of it, press it flat between your palms and place on the filling. Fit the pieces together as you would a jigsaw and then draw the edges together and smooth over the surface. Wet your hands and press the mixture well down over the filling.

4 Wet a sharp knife and run it around the edge of the dish. Cut the kibbeh into diamond shapes. Place a small dab of butter on each diamond and pour the oil and water over the top. Bake in an oven preheated to 375°F, 190°C, Gas Mark 5 for 30–40 minutes until golden brown and crisp around the edges.

Variation:

Kibbit batata bi-sanieh – potato kibbeh

This is a meatless version of the recipe above.

Filling:
180ml (6fl oz) oil
2 large onions, thinly sliced

Kibbeh:
Use the kibbeh recipe given in Kibbeh-bil-sanieh, but replace the 350g (12oz) meat with 350g (12oz) mashed potato.

1 Heat half the oil in a frying pan, add the onions and fry until soft. Spread them, with the oil in which they were cooked, over the base of a shallow ovenproof dish about 25cm (10″) in diameter.

2 Prepare the kibbeh as described above, using the mashed

potato instead of the meat. Keeping your hands damp spread the potato kibbeh mixture evenly over the onions. Press the mixture down well and smooth over the surface.

3 Wet a sharp knife and run it around the edge of the dish. Cut the kibbeh into diamonds and pour the remaining oil over the top. Cook in an oven preheated to 375°F, 190°C, Gas mark 5 for about 30 minutes or until crisp and golden.

Kabat al batatis min bourghul – potato kibbeh with apricot filling

This unusual filling of meat and apricots is a favourite of the people of Iraqi Kurdistan.

These delicious kibbehs are fried in oil and served with fresh vegetables.

Filling:
3 tablespoons ghee or oil
1 large onion, finely chopped
450g (1lb) minced meat
3 tablespoons chopped almonds or hazelnuts
175g (6oz) dried apricots, chopped
½ teaspoon cumin
¼ teaspoon nutmeg
1 teaspoon paprika
1½ teaspoons salt
½ teaspoon black pepper
6 tablespoons water

Kibbeh:
675g (1½lb) mashed potato
175g (6oz) fine burghul, washed in bowl or sieve until water runs
  clear, then drained
40g (1½oz) plain flour
1 large egg
2 teaspoons salt
¾ teaspoon black pepper
3 tablespoons water

To cook:
Oil for frying

Garnish:
Fresh vegetables e.g. radishes, cucumber, tomatoes, lettuce etc.

1 First prepare the filling by heating the ghee or oil in a pan, adding the onion and frying until soft. Add the meat and fry for 10–15 minutes, stirring frequently to break up the lumps. Add the remaining ingredients, mix well and cook for about 30 minutes or until the meat is cooked. Set aside to cool.

2 Place all the kibbeh ingredients in a large bowl and knead for 5–10 minutes.

3 Break off lumps of the kibbeh mixture and form into balls about 4cm (1½″) in diameter. Taking one ball at a time, and keeping your hands damp, hold it in the palm of one hand and push the forefinger of the other hand into the centre. Press all around the wall while rotating the ball slowly and evenly. Continue until the walls are as thin as possible. Place a tablespoon of the filling in the opening, lightly moisten your hands and draw the edges together and seal tightly. Roll the ball between your palms to give it a round, smooth shape and then press gently between your palms to flatten slightly. Reserve and continue until you have used up all the ingredients.

4 Heat sufficient oil in a large saucepan to deep-fry, add the kibbeh, a few at a time and fry gently for 8–10 minutes until evenly golden. Remove with a slotted spoon, drain and keep warm while you cook the remaining kibbeh in the same way. Serve hot with fresh vegetables.

Kibbeh laqtin – pumpkin and burghul in a tray

In this recipe pumpkin and burghul are mixed together and cooked in the oven. You can substitute the pumpkin with vegetable marrows, courgettes or aubergines.

Filling:
2 large onions, thinly sliced
180ml (6fl oz) oil

Kibbeh:

450g (1lb) pumpkin flesh, cubed
350g (12oz) fine burghul, washed in bowl or sieve until water runs
  clear then drained
1 medium onion, very finely chopped
1½ teaspoons salt
1 teaspoon black pepper
3 tablespoons flour
½ teaspoon chilli pepper
1 teaspoon cumin
2 tablespoons finely chopped coriander or mint OR 2 teaspoons dried
  coriander or mint

1 Heat half the oil in a frying pan, add the onions and fry until
soft. Spread them, with the oil in which they were cooked, over
the base of a shallow ovenproof dish about 25cm (10″) in
diameter.
2 Meanwhile cook the pumpkin in lightly salted boiling water
until tender. Drain well and either mash with a fork or purée
in a blender.
3 Spread the burghul out on a baking sheet and knead for a
few minutes. Add the pumpkin and all the remaining
ingredients and knead for about 10 minutes. Sprinkle in a
little more flour if necessary.
4 Keeping your hands damp, spread the kibbeh mixture
evenly over the onions. Press down firmly and smooth over the
surface. Wet a sharp knife and run it around the edge of the
dish. Cut the kibbeh into diamonds and pour the remaining oil
over the top. Cook in an oven preheated to 375°F, 190°C, Gas
Mark 5 for about 30 minutes or until crisp and golden.

Madzounov kufta – kibbeh in yoghurt sauce

A classic Middle Eastern dish popular throughout Turkey,
Syria and Armenia. You can use the meat and onion filling or
the suet filling (page 133) or you can cook the kibbeh 'blind' i.e.
without a filling.
  Serve in soup bowls with bread.

Filling:
Prepare the filling of your choice.

Kibbeh:
Prepare it as described in the recipe for Amram (page 131).

Sauce:
1 × 1.5kg (2–3lb) chicken, jointed
2 teaspoons salt
110g (4oz) chickpeas, soaked overnight in cold water and drained
1.5l (2½ pints) yoghurt
2 eggs
50g (2oz) butter
1 tablespoon dried mint

1 Half fill a large saucepan with water, add the chicken pieces,
salt and chickpeas and bring to the boil. Remove any scum
which appears on the surface and cook until chicken and
chickpeas are tender.
2 If using a suet filling remove it from the refrigerator and
make it into small pea-sized balls.
3 If making 'blind' kufta simply break off small pieces of the
kibbeh mixture and roll into marble-sized balls. Keep your
hands damp while working.
4 If stuffing the kufta, break off a piece of kibbeh about the
size of a small walnut and roll into a ball. Push your forefinger
into the centre and then, holding it so that your forefinger is
parallel to the palm of the other hand, press your finger down
into the kibbeh thus making it thinner. Slowly rotate the ball
in the palm of your hand all the while pressing down with your
forefinger making the shell of the ball uniformly thinner. Put a
ball of suet or a teaspoon of the meat and onion filling into the
hole. Bring the edges of the opening together and seal. Dampen
your hands and roll the ball between your palms to give it a
round shape and smooth surface. Repeat until you have used
up all the ingredients.
5 Mix the yoghurt and eggs together in a bowl, add a little of
the hot chicken stock and stir well. Pour the yoghurt sauce into
the large pan of stock with the chicken and chickpeas. Bring to

simmering point, add the kufta balls and simmer very gently for 10–15 minutes until cooked.

6 Meanwhile melt the butter in a small pan, add the mint, stir and pour into the soup. Serve the dish hot by placing several kufta in a soup bowl with some of the chicken and chickpeas and plenty of the sauce.

Ttoo kufta – sour meat and kibbeh stew

A delicious stew of meat, chickpeas and kibbeh balls. You can add pumpkin, courgettes or aubergines to give it even more substance, but it makes a fine meal as it is.

Serve with bread or a plain rice or burghul pilav.

Kibbeh:
See the ingredients for Amram (page 131).

Sauce:
4 tablespoons oil
2 large onions, thinly sliced
350g (12oz) lamb, cut into 1cm (½″) pieces
175g (6oz) chickpeas, soaked overnight in cold water and drained
3 tablespoons tomato purée
2 teaspoons salt
1 teaspoon black pepper
2 cloves garlic, crushed
1 tablespoon dried mint
3 tablespoons lemon juice

1 Heat the oil in a large saucepan, add the onions and meat and fry for about 5 minutes, turning frequently. Add the chickpeas and plenty of water and bring to the boil. Lower the heat and simmer for 45–60 minutes or until the chickpeas and meat are tender. Remove any scum that appears on the surface.

2 Stir in the remaining sauce ingredients and simmer for a further 20–30 minutes. Taste and adjust seasoning if necessary.

3 Prepare the kibbeh as described in the recipe for Amram. These kufta are cooked 'blind' i.e. without a filling. To make

them, dampen your hands, break off small pieces of the kibbeh mixture and roll between your palms to form small, marble-sized balls.

4   When completed add the kufta to the sauce and simmer gently for about 30 minutes.

5   Serve in soup bowls with bread, or as a main dish with a pilav.

Kharperti kufta – stuffed kibbeh in tomato sauce

A classic kibbeh dish from Southern Turkey. It is tasty and filling.

Kibbeh:
See the ingredients for Amram (page 131).

Filling:
3 tablespoons ghee
1 large onion, finely chopped
350g (¾lb) minced meat
1 large green pepper, seeded and chopped
3 tablespoons finely chopped parsley
1 teaspoon dried basil
1 teaspoon salt
½ teaspoon black pepper
1 level teaspoon cinnamon
4 tablespoons chopped walnuts

Sauce:
1.8l (3 pints) stock or water
3 tablespoons tomato purée
1½ teaspoons salt
1 teaspoon dried mint

1   First prepare the filling by melting the ghee in a saucepan. Add the onion and fry until soft. Add the meat and green pepper and fry for about 30 minutes or until the meat is cooked, stirring frequently. Add the remaining ingredients, stir well and set aside to cool.

2   Prepare the kibbeh mixture as described in the recipe for

Amram (page 131). Break off lumps of the kibbeh and roll into
balls about 4cm (1½″) in diameter.

3 To stuff the kibbeh take one of the balls and, keeping your
hands damp, hold it in the palm of one hand and push the
forefinger of the other hand into the centre. Press all round the
wall while rotating the ball slowly and evenly. Continue until
the walls are as thin as possible. Place a tablespoon of the
filling in the opening, lightly moisten your hands, draw the
edges together and seal tightly. Roll the ball between your
palms to give it a round and smooth shape and then press
gently between your palms to flatten slightly. Set aside and
continue until you have used up all the ingredients.

4 Bring the water or stock to the boil in a large saucepan and
stir in the tomato purée, salt and dried mint. Add the kufta and
cook for 10–15 minutes, or until they rise to the surface.

5 Serve a few kufta in each soup bowl with some of the sauce.

Kibbeh hali – Alouite kibbeh

A lovely dish, full of the flavours of the countryside. It is a
classic from Northern Syria, especially the region of Latakia
where the Alouite sect are based.

Kibbeh:
350g (12oz) fine burghul, washed in bowl or sieve until water runs
  clear, then drained
175g (6oz) plain flour or fine matzo meal or oatmeal
2 small eggs

Sauce:
6 tablespoons oil
1 large onion, finely chopped
3 cloves garlic, finely chopped
1½ tablespoons ground coriander
4 tablespoons tomato purée diluted in 450ml (¾ pint) water
2 teaspoons salt
3 bay leaves
1 level teaspoon allspice

1 teaspoon chilli pepper
1 teaspoon black pepper
1.2l (2 pints) water or stock
Juice of 1 large lemon

Garnish:
3 tablespoons finely chopped parsley

1 Spread the burghul out on a baking tray and knead for a few
minutes. Add the flour, matzo meal or oatmeal and the eggs.
Mix everything together and then knead until you have a
paste thick enough to mould. If you find the mixture a little
sticky then leave for about 15 minutes to enable the burghul to
absorb the extra moisture.
2 Keeping your hands damp, shape teaspoons of the mixture
into small balls about the size of marbles. Set these balls aside
while you prepare the sauce.
3 Heat the oil in a saucepan, add the onion and fry until soft
and lightly browned. Add the garlic and coriander and fry for a
further 2 minutes, stirring frequently. Add the diluted tomato
purée, salt, bay leaves, allspice, chilli and black peppers and
the water and stir well. Bring to the boil, add the kibbeh balls
and simmer for about 30 minutes or until the sauce thickens.
Stir in the lemon juice.
4 Transfer to a large dish, sprinkle with the parsley and serve.

Nourov kufta – kibbeh in pomegranate sauce

'Eat a pomegranate and visit a bath (Turkish bath), your youth will
haste back.' – *Egyptian saying*

Concentrated pomegranate syrup can be bought from some
oriental stores. It is rather expensive, although it will last for a
long time. If you wish you could prepare your own and for this
reason a recipe can be found in the Glossary (page 227).

Kibbeh:
See ingredients for Amram (page 131).

Sauce:
1 tablespoon flour
600ml (1 pint) water

600ml (1 pint) pomegranate juice OR 4 tablespoons pomegranate
  syrup diluted in 600ml (1 pint) water

Garnish:
25g (1oz) butter
2 cloves garlic, finely chopped
3 tablespoons finely chopped coriander or parsley

1 Prepare the kibbeh as described in the recipe for Amram
(page 131). These kuftas are cooked 'blind' i.e. without a filling.
To make them, dampen your hands, break off small pieces of
the kibbeh mixture and roll between your palms to form small,
marble-sized balls.
2 To prepare the sauce first mix the flour to a smooth paste
with some of the water. Pour into a large saucepan and stir in
the remaining water and the pomegranate juice. Bring gently
to the boil, stirring constantly. Add the kufta and simmer for
20–30 minutes.
3 Meanwhile melt the butter in a small pan, add the garlic
and coriander or parsley and fry for about 2 minutes, stirring
frequently.
4 When the kuftas are cooked stir the butter mixture into the
large pan. Remove from the heat, transfer to a large dish and
serve with a rice or burghul pilav.

Kibbi arnabieh – kibbeh in tahina sauce

The combination of tahina with citrus juices gives this
Lebanese favourite a unique flavour that more than
compensates for the preparation time.
   A rich and filling dish.

Filling:
See ingredients for Meat and onion filling (page 133).

Kibbeh:
See ingredients for Amram (page 131).

Stew:
450g (1lb) shoulder of lamb, cut into 2.5cm (1″) pieces
1½ teaspoons salt

1 level teaspoon allspice
5cm (2") cinnamon stick
50g (2oz) butter
1 large onion, thinly sliced
200ml (⅓ pint) tahina
Juice of 2 grapefruit, 2 lemons and 2 oranges
110g (4oz) chickpeas, soaked overnight in cold water, drained and
  cooked until tender

1 Prepare the meat and onion filling according to the recipe on
page 133.
2 Prepare the kibbeh as described in the recipe for Amram.
3 Fill small kibbeh balls by following instruction 4 in the
recipe for Madzounov kufta. Refrigerate the kibbeh balls while
you prepare the stew.
4 Place the meat in a saucepan with the salt, allspice,
cinnamon and enough water to cover by at least 5cm (2"). Bring
to the boil, lower the heat, cover the pan and simmer for about
45–60 minutes or until the meat is tender.
5 Remove the meat with a slotted spoon and reserve. It can
either be served separately in a side dish or returned to the
stew 10 minutes before serving. Measure the stock and make
up to 1.2l (2 pints) if necessary.
6 Melt the butter in a large saucepan, add the onion and fry
until soft.
7 Meanwhile mix the tahina with the fruit juices in a small
bowl and, if necessary add sufficient water to make a thin,
creamy consistency. Pour this mixture into the pan with the
onions and add the 1.2l (2 pints) of stock and the cooked
chickpeas. Bring gently to the boil, stirring frequently.
8 Add the kibbeh balls and simmer for about 30 minutes.
Transfer to a large dish and serve with a plain pilav.

Kibbeh-bil-samak – fish kibbeh

Another Lebanese speciality.
   This dish is similar to Kibbeh-bil-sanieh (page 137), but fish
replaces the meat. Any firm, white fish will do, e.g. halibut, cod
or coley.

Serve with a bowl of salad.

Filling:
150ml (¼ pint) oil
2 onions, thinly sliced
75g (3oz) pine kernels or coarsely chopped walnuts

Kibbeh:
250g (9oz) fine burghul, washed in bowl or sieve until water runs
   clear, then drained
350g (12oz) white fish, skin and bones discarded, minced
1 medium onion, very finely chopped
1 tablespoon sweet basil
Grated rind of 1 orange
1 teaspoon salt
½ teaspoon black pepper

To cook:
Pinch allspice
4–5 tablespoons oil

1 Prepare the filling by heating the 150ml (¼ pint) oil in a
small pan. Add the onions and fry until soft. Add the nuts and
fry for a further 2–3 minutes. Remove from the heat and
reserve.
2 Spread the burghul out on a baking tray and leave for a few
minutes.
3 Meanwhile mix the remaining kibbeh ingredients together
well in a bowl and then add to the burghul. Dampen your
hands and knead for about 10 minutes.
4 Lightly grease a shallow baking dish about 25cm (10″) in
diameter and sprinkle the base with a little allspice. Spread
half the burghul mixture evenly over the bottom of the dish.
Spread the filling over this. Now arrange the remaining
burghul mixture over the top. The easiest way to do this is to
break off lumps of kibbeh, press them flat between your palms
and place over the filling. Fit the pieces together like a jigsaw
and then draw the edges together and smooth over. Wet your
hands and press the mixture down firmly.
5 Wet a sharp knife and run it around the edge of the dish. Cut

into diamond shapes and pour the oil evenly over the top. Bake in an oven preheated to 375°F, 190°C, Gas mark 5 for 30–40 minutes or until golden.

Wheat

'Everything is rubbish except wheat and wool.' (food and clothing) –
Arabian saying

The cultivation of wheat (*Triticum*) reaches far back into
history. It was cultivated in Persia, Anatolia, Egypt, Greece
and finally Europe, where it arrived – according to Herodotus –
with the Gauls on one of their many Mediterranean
expeditions. Indeed, wheat was not widespread in Europe until
very late; up to the seventeenth century, the poor had the
choice of either rye or barley bread while in the Middle East
wheaten bread was standard fare well over a thousand years
before.

Wheat has almost always been cultivated for the making of
bread. I say 'almost' because there are still some regions of the
world where wheat in its 'whole-grain' form is still used to
prepare soups, salads, pilavs and desserts. Naturally, in days
past, it was in much wider use, but the arrival of rice from the
Far East has changed the balance so much that today
whole-grain wheat has all but disappeared from most Western
kitchens.

Wheat is grown throughout the world from the borders of the
Arctic to near the Equator, although the crop is most
successful between the latitudes 30°N–60°N and 27°S–40°S. It
grows best on heavy loam and clay, although it makes a
satisfactory crop on lighter soil. The seed is sown in late
autumn (winter wheat) or in spring (spring wheat). There are
literally thousands of known species and varieties of the genus
Triticum. Common or bread wheat is called *Triticum aestivum*
and this is the grain that interests us. This grain consists of
three parts: shell (pericarp), nut (caryopsis) and seed (embryo).
Wheat grains contain gluten, starch and also nitrogenous
matter and fats, sugar, dextrines and mineral salt (ash).

The two basic classifications are a) hard grain – rich in
gluten and b) soft grain – rich in starch. Apart from flour, and
hence bread, wheat is also used in the manufacture of cereals
and pasta. From wheat grains are also prepared burghul (page
111), cous-cous (page 229), tarkana (page 230) and polenta
(page 230). Simply put, wheat is a delicious alternative to rice
and can be treated as such.

The simplest method of preparation, and one that is still practised in many agriculturally-based societies today, is to make a porridge-type meal by soaking one part wheat grains in three parts water for 6–8 hours and then boiling until the grains are tender. The cooking time, much longer than rice, is usually 1½–1¾ hours.

The first recipe is a simple kasha from Eastern Europe. Prepare it as an alternative to a rice pilav or, indeed, to any other accompaniment to your main dish of the day.

Pshyenitzaya kasha – whole wheat kasha

350g (12oz) whole wheat grains, washed and drained
1.8l (3 pints) water
1½ teaspoons salt

1 Place the wheat and water in a large bowl and leave for 6–8 hours.
2 Pour the contents of the bowl into a large saucepan and bring to the boil. Cover the pan and cook over a moderate heat for 30 minutes, stirring occasionally.
3 Lower the heat further and cook for a further 1½ hours or until the grains are soft and puffed up and the liquid has been absorbed. Ten minutes before the end of the cooking time stir in the salt.

Variation: substitute the water with the same quantity of milk, but omit the salt.

Whole wheat pilav

This makes an ideal substitute for rice. Indeed, you can treat it as rice with the addition of butter, salt, pepper, as well as such vegetables as onion, tomatoes, garlic, peppers etc. In short, this dish is open to much experimentation. Serve as an accompaniment to any meat, fish or poultry dish of your choice.

350g (12oz) whole grain wheat, washed and drained
1.8l (3 pints) water
75g (3oz) butter

1 large onion, thinly sliced
2 cloves garlic, crushed
1½ teaspoons salt
½ teaspoon black pepper
½ teaspoon chilli pepper
3 tablespoons finely chopped parsley

1 Place the whole wheat and water in a large bowl and leave
to soak for 6–8 hours.
2 Pour the contents of the bowl into a large saucepan and
bring to the boil. Cover the pan and cook over a moderate heat
for 30 minutes, stirring occasionally.
3 Meanwhile melt the butter in a small pan, add the onion and
garlic and fry until soft. Add the seasonings and parsley and
mix well.
4 At the end of the 30 minutes stir the onion mixture into the
whole wheat. Lower the heat and cook for a further 1½ hours
or until the grains are soft and puffed up and the liquid has
been absorbed.
5 Remove from the heat, set aside for 10 minutes and then
serve.

Parinji pilav – whole wheat with almonds and raisins
'Parinji' is the local Caucasian dialect for wheat.
This is a filling dish. Serve with salad and yoghurt or as an
accompaniment to grilled meats and kebabs.

350g (12oz) whole wheat
1.8l (3 pints) water
1½ teaspoons salt
50g (2oz) butter
1 onion, finely chopped
50g (2oz) vermicelli, broken into 2.5cm (1″) pieces
3 cloves
2 bay leaves
50g (2oz) raisins
50g (2oz) slivered almonds
3 tablespoons finely chopped parsley
1 teaspoon dried basil

Garnish:
1 teaspoon paprika
2–3 spring onions, including the green heads, thinly sliced

1 Place the wheat and water in a large bowl and leave for
6–8 hours.
2 Pour the contents of the bowl into a large saucepan and
bring to the boil. Cover the pan and cook over a moderate heat
for 30 minutes, stirring occasionally.
3 Meanwhile melt the butter in a small pan, add the onion and
fry until soft. Add the vermicelli and fry until golden, stirring
frequently. Stir all the remaining ingredients into the onion
pan. Transfer this mixture to the whole wheat saucepan and
stir well. Cover the pan, lower the heat and cook for a further
1½ hours or until the grains are soft and puffed up and all the
liquid has been absorbed.
4 Remove from the heat and leave for a few minutes before
spooning into a large dish. Sprinkle with the paprika and
chopped spring onions and serve.

Tahinov tzoreni pilav – whole wheat with tahini sauce

If purslane is not avilable use fresh spinach instead.
    This is a regional dish from Southern Turkey. Serve it on its
own with a bowl of salad, or as an accompaniment to a fish or
poultry dish of your choice.

225g (8oz) whole wheat soaked for 6–8 hours in 1.2l (2 pints) cold
  water
110g (4oz) chickpeas, soaked in cold water for 6–8 hours
175g (6oz) purslane or spinach, washed thoroughly and coarsely
  chopped
1 red or green pepper, seeded and thinly sliced
1 teaspoon dillweed
1½ teaspoons salt
1 teaspoon chilli pepper

Sauce:
90ml (3fl oz) tahina
90ml (3fl oz) water

4 cloves garlic, crushed
½ teaspoon salt

Garnish:
1 teaspoon paprika
3 tablespoons finely chopped parsley or coriander

1 Pour the wheat and its soaking water into a large saucepan
and bring to the boil. Cover the pan and cook over a moderate
heat for 30 minutes.
2 Meanwhile drain the chickpeas and then skin them by
squeezing each one between thumb and forefinger.
3 After the 30 minutes add the chickpeas to the wheat pan,
cover and cook for a further hour.
4 Stir in the purslane or spinach, pepper, dillweed, salt and
chilli pepper and cook for a further 30 minutes or until the
wheat grains and chickpeas are tender and the water has been
absorbed.
5 Remove from the heat and set aside for a few minutes while
you prepare the sauce. Place the tahina, water, garlic and salt
in a small bowl and beat until smooth and creamy.
6 To serve, spoon the pilav into a large dish and dribble half
the sauce over the top. Sprinkle with the paprika and parsley
or coriander and serve the rest of the sauce in a small jug.

Herisseh – lamb with whole wheat

'Wisdom . . . hath killed her beasts; she had mingled her wine; she had
also furnished her table.
She had sent forth her maidens; she crieth upon the highest places of
the city ——
Come, eat of my bread, and drink of the wine which I have mingled.'
(Proverbs 9:2–5)

In the tradition of Wisdom, Christians in the Middle East, on
the feast of St Mary, go to church, slaughter a lamb or chicken
and cook herisseh in large cauldrons. All relations, friends,
friends of friends and strangers passing by are invited to
participate in the feasting. This act of sharing one's food with
strangers goes back to the beginnings of civilisation, as does

this dish of wheat with meat or chicken. Herisseh is one of the oldest dishes known to man. It is perhaps the same as the one Ezekiel recommended to be cooked:

'Set on a pot, set it on, and also pour water into it. Gather the pieces thereof into it, even every good pieces, the thigh and the shoulder; fill it with the choice bones – and make it boil well. Heap on wood, kindle the fire, consume the flesh, and spice it well.' *(Ezekiel 24:3–10)*

From Morocco to Arabia and north to the Caucasus, as well as in the Greek Islands, a dish of wheat cooked with spices and meat has survived the vagaries of time. Below are two versions of this ancient dish. The first is from the mountains of Lebanon and best when served with a bowl of fresh yoghurt.

450g (1lb) whole wheat, soaked in 2.5l (4 pints) water for 6–8 hours
1kg (2lb) lean lamb, cut into 2.5cm (1") pieces
5cm (2") piece cinnamon stick
2 teaspoons salt
1 teaspoon black pepper

Garnish:
A little olive oil

1 Pour the wheat and soaking water into a large saucepan and add the pieces of meat. Bring to the boil, reduce the heat to moderate and cook for 30 minutes. Remove any scum that appears on the surface.
2 Add the cinnamon stick, salt and black pepper. Cover the pan, lower the heat further and simmer for 1½–2 hours or until most of the liquid had been absorbed. During and after cooking mash frequently until the mixture has the consistency of a thick porridge.
3 Spoon the mixture into a large dish and dribble some olive oil over the surface. Serve with yoghurt and a salad. Serves 6–8.

Variation: Chicken with whole wheat

In this recipe burghul or pearl barley can be used instead of wheat, but these grains do not require prior soaking and need only half the stated amount of water and half the cooking time.

450g (1lb) whole wheat, soaked in 2.5l (4 pints) water for 6–8 hours
1 × 1.5–1.75kg (3–4lb) chicken, jointed
2 teaspoons salt
1 teaspoon black pepper
1 heaped teaspoon cinnamon

Garnish:
75g (3oz) butter
1½ teaspoons paprika
2 heaped teaspoons cumin

1 Pour the wheat and soaking water into a large saucepan and
add the chicken pieces. Bring to the boil, reduce the heat to
moderate and cook for 30 minutes. Remove any scum that
appears on the surface.
2 Cover the pan, lower the heat further and cook for another
1½–2 hours or until most of the liquid has been absorbed.
After 30 minutes of this cooking time, remove the chicken
pieces, if tender. When cool enough to handle, strip the flesh
from the bones, shred it finely and return to the pan. While the
mixture is cooking mash it frequently to obtain a thick
porridge.
3 Melt the butter in a small saucepan and stir in the paprika.
4 To serve spoon the herisseh into individual soup bowls.
Spoon a little of the butter mixture over each portion and
sprinkle with cumin.
    Serves 6–8.

Bugday pilavi etli – wheat, meat and tomato pilav

A popular dish from the remote parts of Anatolia where it is
served with a bowl of yoghurt. I suggest you also add a plain
Shepherd's Salad (page 223).

450g (1lb) whole wheat, soaked in 2.5l (4 pints) water for 6–8 hours
50g (2oz) butter
2 large onions, coarsely chopped
450g (1lb) lean lamb, cut into 2.5cm (1″) pieces
2 large tomatoes, blanched, peeled and chopped
1 tablespoon tomato purée

1½ teaspoons salt
½ teaspoon black pepper
1 teaspoon curry powder
2 bay leaves
600ml (1 pint) water

1 Pour the wheat and its soaking water into a large saucepan and bring to the boil. Reduce the heat to moderate and cook for 30 minutes.
2 Cover the pan, lower the heat further and simmer for another 1½ hours or until the wheat is soft and puffed up.
3 Meanwhile melt the butter in a saucepan, add the onions and fry until soft, stirring frequently. Add the meat cubes and fry for 5–10 minutes, turning regularly. Stir in the tomatoes, tomato purée, salt, pepper, curry powder, bay leaves and half the water. Bring to the boil, cover the pan, lower the heat and simmer for about 45 minutes.
4 Stir the rest of the water into the meat mixture and stir it into the wheat pan for the last 30–45 minutes of its cooking time.
5 Set aside for a few minutes and then serve.

Kasha

Under the general heading of Kasha I have included
buckwheat, barley, millet and rye recipes because, in Russian,
'kasha' simply means 'cereal'. This is regardless of whether it
is boiled or steamed as porridge or gruel, or steamed or baked
as a pilav.

For centuries, to the ordinary Russian, cabbage or beetroot
soup and kasha were all that was available. Even today rice is
little used outside the Central Asian and Caucasian Republics,
while wheat, i.e. burghul, is unknown beyond the borders of
the Armenian Republic.

Traditionally kasha was prepared in large stoves, but today
it is often cooked like rice.

Buckwheat

Buckwheat is little used in Britain and Western Europe. It
comes to the fore in the diet of the people of Eastern Europe.

Buckwheat – *Fagopyrum* – is a genus annual herbaceous
plant of the *Polygoniaceae* family, related to rhubarbs and
sorrels. The stems are bare and branching, the leaves alternate
and triangular. The flowers have short styles with long
stamens and long styles with short stamens. The fruit is
nut-like in appearance. Buckwheat grows well in humus-rich
soil and cultivated peat bogs. It is cultivated for its grain which
is processed to make groats and flour. The bi-products of the
seeds – husks, farina, straw and chaff – are used for fodder.

Cultivated buckwheat originated in the mountainous
regions of India and the Himalayas about 4000 years ago. It
was introduced into Europe in the 19th century.

Buckwheat is extensively cultivated in Eastern Europe –
Poland and the USSR – and also in France, Germany and
Canada. In Britain it is, to date, only used as animal fodder. It
is full of essential amino acids, riboflavin, potassium, iron and
thiamine.

Buckwheat plays a major role in the cuisine of Russia, and it
is to the Steppes of that vast continent we must go for the most
interesting buckwheat-based recipes. Buckwheat can be

bought at most good health food shops. Like burghul (page 109) it comes in three grades, fine, medium and coarse. I suggest you use only the coarse grade.

The first recipe is for a plain buckwheat kasha casserole which can be served as it is as an accompaniment to meat and/or vegetable dishes, but which is also used as the basis for several of the following dishes.

Gryechnyevaya kasha – buckwheat casserole

350g (12oz) buckwheat grains, black grains discarded
1 teaspoon salt
600ml (1 pint) boiling water
50g (2oz) butter

1 Place the kasha in a heavy-based saucepan and cook over a medium heat for 5 minutes, stirring constantly, until the grains have darkened and are toasted.
2 Lightly grease an ovenproof casserole and add the toasted kasha to it. Sprinkle with the salt and pour in the boiling water. Dot with the butter and cover the dish. Place in an oven preheated to 350°F, 180°C, Gas Mark 4 and cook for about 45 minutes.
3 Remove from the oven and serve with meat, poultry or fish dishes. If you wish you can pour a little extra melted butter over it before serving.

NB This dish can also be cooked in the saucepan on top of the cooker. In this case the cooking time is about 20–30 minutes.

Variations: Slight variations can be achieved with the minimum of effort. Try
a) Beating one egg, adding to the pan with the buckwheat and stirring until each grain is well coated. Cook over a medium heat for 5 minutes, stirring all the time to ensure that all the egg is absorbed. When the grains are toasted proceed as above.
b) Fry a chopped onion in 50g (2oz) butter in a small pan until soft and then add to the toasted buckwheat and proceed as above.

c) Add 2 tablespoons chopped fresh dill to the boiling water and proceed as above.

Gryechnyevaya kasha so shpikom-i-lukom – buckwheat kasha with salt pork and onions

Ingredients as for the Buckwheat casserole above plus:
50g (2oz) butter
1 large onion, chopped
350g (12oz) salt pork (see Glossary), cut into 0.5cm (¼″) cubes

1 Prepare the buckwheat casserole as described above.
2 Meanwhile melt the butter in a pan, add the onion and salt pork and fry for 5–7 minutes, or until the onion is soft.
3 When the kasha is cooked stir the onion and salt pork into it and leave over a low heat for a further 5 minutes before serving.

Gryechnyevaya kasha s-mozramou – buckwheat kasha with brains

Makes a filling meal when served with salad, pickles and soured cream or yoghurt.

Ingredients for Buckwheat casserole above plus:
350g (12oz) lamb's or calf's brains
3 tablespoons vinegar
2 tablespoons salt
2 bay leaves
½ teaspoon black pepper
50g (2oz) butter
1 teaspoon dried dillweed
1 teaspoon paprika

1 Place the brains in a large bowl and add enough cold water to cover. Add 2 tablespoons of the vinegar and 1 tablespoon of the salt and leave to soak for 1 hour. Change the water 2–3 times.
2 Remove the brains from the water, rinse and cut away and discard any loose outer membranes.

3 Place the brains in a saucepan, cover with cold water and add the remaining vinegar and salt, the bay leaves and black pepper. Bring to the boil, lower the heat, cover the pan and simmer for 5 minutes. Drain and set the brains aside.

4 Prepare the kasha as described for Buckwheat Casserole above.

5 Meanwhile melt the butter in a small pan. Cut the brains into 1cm (½") pieces and add to the pan. Sprinkle with the dillweed and paprika and fry for 3–4 minutes, stirring regularly. Stir this mixture into the cooked kasha and cook for a further 5 minutes before serving.

Gryechnyevaya kasha s-gryamy-e-lukom – buckwheat kasha with onions and mushrooms

A Russian housewife will only use dried mushrooms for this recipe. Russians, and indeed all the Slav nations, are famed for their rich mushroom-based dishes and general expertise in preserving mushrooms.

If you wish to be authentic I suggest you follow the instructions given in the Glossary (page 227). However, this dish is equally successful and tasty if made with fresh mushrooms.

110g (4oz) dried mushrooms OR 350g (12oz) fresh mushrooms, wiped clean and thinly sliced
50g (2oz) butter
2 large onions, chopped
350g (12oz) buckwheat grains
1 teaspoon salt

1 If using dried mushrooms soak them for 1–1½ hours in cold water. When they have swollen remove them from the water and slice thinly. Reserve the water.

2 Melt the butter in a frying pan, add the onions and fry until soft, stirring regularly. Add the sliced mushrooms and fry for a further 3–4 minutes. Set aside.

3 Place the buckwheat in a heavy-based saucepan and cook

over a medium heat for 5 minutes, stirring constantly, until
the grains have darkened and are toasted. Stir in the
mushrooms and onions.
4 Lightly grease an ovenproof casserole and turn the mixture
into it. Make the mushroom water up to 600ml (1 pint) if
necessary, bring to the boil and pour into the casserole OR add
600ml (1 pint) boiling water. Stir in the salt and cook in an
oven preheated to 350°F, 180°C, Gas Mark 4 for 45 minutes.
5 Remove from the oven and serve with a meat dish or as a
savoury with salad and soured cream or yoghurt.

Gryechnyevaya kasha potrakhalam – buckwheat kasha
with liver

Traditionally the lights, heart, lungs and entrails of sheep or
pig were used for this recipe, but you can use the offal of veal or
beef. Today liver often replaces the offal.

   Makes a tasty, filling meal. Serve with salad and soured
cream or yoghurt.

350g (12oz) lamb's or calf's liver
350g (12oz) buckwheat grains
600ml (1 pint) boiling water
1 teaspoon salt
110g (4oz) butter
1 large onion, thinly sliced
½ teaspoon salt
½ teaspoon black pepper
1 teaspoon dill seed

1 Wash and dry the liver and cut into 0.5cm (¼") pieces. Set
aside.
2 Place the buckwheat in a heavy-based saucepan and cook
over a medium heat for about 5 minutes, stirring constantly,
until the grains have darkened and are toasted.
3 Lightly grease an ovenproof casserole and add the toasted
buckwheat. Stir in the boiling water, salt and half the butter,
cover and cook in an oven heated to 350°F, 180°C, Gas Mark 4
for about 45 minutes.

4 Meanwhile melt the remaining butter in a frying pan, add
the onion and fry until soft. Add the liver, salt, black pepper
and dill seed and fry for about 5 minutes, stirring frequently.
5 Remove the kasha from the oven and stir in the onion and
liver mixture. Return to the oven for a further 5 minutes and
then serve.

Gryechnyevaya kasha ryepam – buckwheat kasha with
turnip

This recipe is also popular in Poland and the Scandinavian
countries. It makes an ideal accompaniment to pork, duck and
particularly wild fowl.

110g (4oz) butter
450g (1lb) turnips, peeled and grated
250g (9oz) buckwheat grains, washed and drained
900ml (1½ pints) milk, boiling
1 tablespoon sugar
½ teaspoon salt

Garnish:
50g (2oz) melted butter (optional)
½ teaspoon black pepper
1 teaspoon paprika

1 Melt half the butter in a large saucepan, add the grated
turnip and fry for 4–5 minutes, stirring regularly. Mix in the
buckwheat and fry for a further 2–3 minutes.
2 Lightly grease a large, ovenproof casserole and turn the
buckwheat mixture into it. Pour in the milk, add the sugar,
salt and remaining butter and mix well. Cover and cook in an
oven preheated to 350°F, 180°C, Gas Mark 4 for about 1½
hours.
3 Remove from the oven and spoon into a large dish. Pour over
the extra melted butter if you wish and then sprinkle with the
black pepper and paprika.

Krupnik – buckwheat with eggs, cheese and soured cream

'Krupnik' means 'grain' or, more precisely, 'small grain'. This in turn comes to mean buckwheat and hence kasha, which neatly brings us to another kasha dish.

This Ukranian recipe is also popular in Poland. It makes a fine savoury meal when served with salads and pickles.

350g (12oz) buckwheat grains
600ml (1 pint) soured cream
1 teaspoon salt
225g (8oz) cottage cheese
3 egg yolks
50g (2oz) butter, softened

1 Place the buckwheat in a saucepan, cover well with water and bring to the boil. Boil over a moderate heat for 2–3 minutes and then drain.
2 Place the soured cream, salt, cheese, egg yolks and butter in a large bowl and beat until well blended. Mix the drained buckwheat in thoroughly.
3 Lightly grease an ovenproof casserole and turn the buckwheat mixture into it. Cover and cook in an oven preheated to 350°F, 180°C, Gas Mark 4 for about 45 minutes. Remove and serve immediately.

Gryechnyevaya kasha kapoustam – buckwheat with cabbage

'Dreaming of grain, the hen scratches the air and falls from her perch.'
– *Avar saying*

This recipe is from the Caucasus on the southern borders of Russia.

Use red cabbage if it is available as it gives extra colour to the dish. It is delicious and goes particularly well with pork. If eating as a main meal, add more variety and texture by stirring in 2 tablespoons each of raisins and coarsely chopped almonds or walnuts.

350g (12oz) buckwheat grains, rinsed and drained
600ml (1 pint) water
50g (2oz) butter
350g (12oz) red or white cabbage, coarsely chopped
2 cloves garlic, crushed
4 spring onions OR 1 small onion, thinly sliced
1 teaspoon salt
½ teaspoon black pepper
1 teaspoon paprika
1 teaspoon thyme

Garnish:
Soured cream

1 Place the buckwheat in a saucepan, add the water and bring
to the boil. Lower the heat, cover the pan and simmer for
30–40 minutes or until the grains are tender, but not mushy.
2 Meanwhile melt the butter in a large saucepan and add the
cabbage, garlic and onion. Fry for 4–5 minutes, stirring
frequently. Add the seasonings and fry for a further 3–4
minutes or until the cabbage is just tender. Set aside.
3 When the kasha is cooked turn it into the cabbage pan and
mix thoroughly. At this stage you can add some raisins and
nuts if you wish. Return the pan to the heat for a few minutes
to heat through and then serve with a little soured cream
spooned over the top.

Kasha cholent – buckwheat stew

225g (8oz) buckwheat
450ml (¾ pint) boiling water
½ teaspoon salt
1 tablespoon butter
3 tablespoons oil
1 large onion, thinly sliced
2 cloves garlic, crushed
1kg (2lb) braising steak or lamb, cut into 4cm (1½″) cubes
110g (4oz) dried white beans e.g. haricot, canellini or butter, soaked
   overnight in cold water
1 teaspoon salt
½ teaspoon black pepper

1 teaspoon paprika
600ml (1 pint) stock or water

1 Place the buckwheat in a heavy-based saucepan and cook
over a medium heat until the grains have darkened and are
toasted, stirring constantly. Turn them into a lightly greased
ovenproof casserole. Add the water, salt and butter, cover and
cook in an oven preheated to 350°F, 180°C, Gas Mark 4 for
30–40 minutes. Remove and set aside.
2 Meanwhile heat the oil in a large casserole. Add the onion
and garlic and fry for a few minutes until the onion is soft. Add
the meat cubes and fry for a few more minutes, stirring
frequently.
3 Drain the beans and add to the pan, together with the salt,
pepper, paprika and stock or water. Mix well and bring to the
boil. Lower the heat, cover the pan and cook for about 1½
hours.
4 Stir in the cooked kasha and cook for a further 45 minutes,
stirring occasionally. If the mixture becomes too dry, add a
little more liquid.
5 Serve immediately.

Gryechnyevaya kotlyeta smetanov – buckwheat rissoles

In our final recipe for buckwheat kasha the grains are mixed
with eggs and shaped into balls or patties. These are then
dredged in breadcrumbs and fried or grilled.
  Serve with soured cream or yoghurt and salads of your
choice.

350g (12oz) buckwheat grains, washed and drained
900ml (1½ pints) water
1 teaspoon salt
1 teaspoon dillweed
3 large egg yolks
2 teaspoons sugar
25g (1oz) butter or dripping
75g (3oz) fresh breadcrumbs
Oil for frying

1 Place the buckwheat grains in a saucepan with the water, salt and dillweed. Bring to the boil, cover the pan, lower the heat and cook over a low heat, stirring occasionally, for about 1 hour or until the kasha is thick and 'porridgey'. Set aside and leave to cool for 15–20 minutes.
2 Beat the egg yolks together and add to the kasha, together with the sugar and butter. Mix together thoroughly.
3 Keeping your hands damp, break off egg-sized lumps and roll into balls. Press between palms to flatten slightly.
4 Heat some oil in a large frying pan. Dip the rissoles in the breadcrumbs and add to the pan, a few at a time, and cook for 5–6 minutes, turning once, until golden and crisp. Remove and keep warm while you fry the rest in the same way.

Barley

'Is it wheat or barley?' – Is it good or bad news? *(Ancient Egyptian expression)*

Grains of barley have been discovered in the Pharaonic tombs of Egypt from the pre-dynastic period, dating from before 6,000BC. Barley is mentioned in the Bible in connection with the numerous plagues of Egypt. It is one of the most ancient cultivated cereals, much used by Sumerians, Hittites, Greeks and Romans – but always as second fiddle to wheat, hence the expression above. For barley grain is poorer in gluten than wheat and its flour does not form an elastic paste like wheat. Barley was the food of the Roman gladiators who were known as the *hordearii* (barley people)!

Barley is grown in temperate climates, mainly as a spring crop, and has a geographic distribution generally similar to that of wheat. However, it has an added attraction since it grows on well-drained soils which need not be as fertile as those required by wheat.

Barley, from the species *hordeum sativum* or *h. vulgare*, has three main classifications:
a) hulled, two-row, grown mainly in Europe, Australia and

the United Kingdom, where it is at its best in light and
medium soils with prevailing moderate temperature and
rainfall.
b) hulled, six-row, is predominant in India and the Middle
East.
c) hull-less barley, is extensively cultivated in South-East
Asia.
'Hulled' refers to the husk which still adheres to the kernel
after threshing, while 'hull-less' suggests that the husk is loose
and can be easily removed during threshing. 'Two' or 'six' row
refers to the arrangement of the grains on the spike. The grain
of barley is spindle-shaped, thicker in the centre and tapering
towards each end.
    In Europe, today, barley is little used in baking bread. Its
main uses are as animal fodder, in the manufacture of beer, in
the distilling of whisky and as an infusion (barley water).
    In other parts of the world barley is still much used as food
for human consumption. It is consumed ground, as porridge, its
flour is used in making flat breads and whole grains are used to
make pilavs, soups and stews.
    In the vast expanses of Eastern Europe and Asia barley
comes to the fore, with buckwheat and millet, as a major cereal
not only as animal fodder, but also for human consumption and
some of the simplest, but not necessarily the least tasty, are
the Kashas of Mother Russia.

Yachnyevaya kasha so svinim ili baranium salom – barley
with pork or mutton suet

Here the barley grains are cooked to a porridge consistency
then mixed with fried suet cracklings and served either for
breakfast or, with salads, pickles and bread, as a nourishing
savoury meal.

350g (12oz) pearl barley, rinsed thoroughly under cold water and
    drained
1.2l (2 pints) water
1 teaspoon salt

40g (1½oz) butter
110g (4oz) raw pork or mutton suet

1 Place the barley, water, salt and butter in a large saucepan
and bring to the boil. Lower the heat, cover the pan and cook
for 50–60 minutes, stirring occasionally.
2 Meanwhile cut the suet into small pieces. Place them in a
small frying pan and fry over a moderate heat for a few
minutes until brown and crisp.
3 When the barley is cooked pour the crackling and fat into it,
mix well and cook over a low heat for a further 10 minutes.
Serve hot.

Peyerlovaya kasha s-maslom – pearl barley with butter

Serve as an accompaniment to grilled meat or chicken dishes.

350g (12oz) pearl barley, rinsed thoroughly under cold water and
   drained
900ml (1½ pints) water
1 teaspoon salt
1 teaspoon dillweed
110g (4oz) butter

1 Place the barley in a saucepan, cover generously with
boiling water and boil for 5 minutes. Drain into a sieve.
2 Place the 900ml (1½ pints) water in a saucepan with the
salt, dillweed and half the butter. Bring to the boil. Add the
drained barley, cover the pan, reduce the heat to low and cook
for 30–40 minutes, stirring occasionally.
3 When all the water has been absorbed and the grains are
tender stir the remaining butter into the kasha and cook over a
low heat for a further 10 minutes. Remove from the heat and
serve.

Yechnyevaya kasha c-smetanom – pearly barley in soured cream

You can serve this kasha with grilled or roast meats, but it also
makes a healthy vegetarian meal in its own right.

1.2l (2 pints) milk
350g (12oz) pearl barley, rinsed thoroughly under cold water and
  drained
25g (1oz) butter
1 teaspoon salt
300ml (½ pint) soured cream
1 large egg

Garnish:
2 tablespoons melted butter
½ teaspoon white pepper

1 Pour the milk into a large saucepan and bring to the boil.
Add the barley, butter and salt and mix thoroughly. Lower the
heat and simmer for 20 minutes, stirring occasionally. Cover
the pan and cook for a further 40 minutes.
2 In a small bowl beat the soured cream and egg together and
stir into the kasha.
3 Lightly grease a casserole and pour the kasha into it. Cook
in an oven preheated to 350°F, 180°C, Gas Mark 4 for a further
20 minutes.
4 Remove from the oven and garnish with the butter and
pepper. Serve immediately.

Vitebskaya kasha – pearl barley with potatoes

A filling casserole which is cooked in the oven. You can mash
the potatoes if you wish, but I prefer them sliced.

1.5kg (3lb) potatoes, scrubbed
225g (8oz) pearl barley, rinsed thoroughly under cold water and
  drained
2 teaspoons salt
1 teaspoon black pepper
1 teaspoon dillweed
600ml (1 pint) milk
50g (2oz) butter, melted

Garnish:
25g (1oz) melted butter (optional)

1 Half fill a large saucepan with lightly salted water and bring

to the boil. Add the scrubbed potatoes and cook until just tender. Drain and peel when cool enough to handle. Mash or slice them thinly.

2 Place the barley in a saucepan, cover with water and bring to the boil. Simmer for 10 minutes and then drain.

3 Generously butter an ovenproof casserole. Layer half the potatoes over the base and sprinkle with half the salt and pepper. Spread the barley evenly over them and sprinkle with the dillweed. Arrange the remaining potatoes over the top and sprinkle with the remaining salt and pepper. Pour in the milk and then brush the top of the potatoes with the melted butter, pouring in any that is left over.

4 Place in an oven preheated to 350°F, 180°C, Gas Mark 4 and bake for 1 hour or until the potatoes are golden.

5 Remove from the oven and serve, sprinkling with the extra melted butter if you wish.

Glazatkaya kasha – pearl barley with peas

'A barley corn is better than a diamond to a rooster' – *American saying*

With this Byelorussian kasha, dried peas were traditionally used. However fresh ones are equally successful.

This dish can be served as a pilav accompanying meat, or as a savoury meal with pork crackling, salad and pickles. I like frying a few rashers of chopped bacon with the onion when preparing this dish. It is delicious and makes a satisfying meal.

350g (12oz) pearl barley, rinsed thoroughly under cold water and drained
50g (2oz) butter
1 large onion, chopped
175g (6oz) dried peas, soaked for 3–4 hours, drained and cooked until tender OR 350g (12oz) fresh or frozen peas
1½ teaspoons salt
1½ teaspoons thyme
900ml (1½ pints) boiling water

Garnish:
25g (1oz) melted butter (optional)

1 Place the pearl barley in a saucepan, cover with water and bring to the boil. Simmer for 10–15 minutes and then drain.
2 Meanwhile melt the butter in a large saucepan and add the onion. Fry until soft, stirring occasionally. Add the peas, drained barley, salt, thyme and boiling water. Lower the heat, cover the pan and cook for about 45 minutes or until the liquid has been absorbed and the barley is tender.
3 Spoon the kasha into a serving dish, dribble the butter over it and serve.

NB If you wish you can prepare this recipe in a casserole and cook it in an oven preheated to 350°F, 180°C, Gas Mark 4 for 45–60 minutes.

At the southern tip of Russia lie the mighty peaks of the Caucasus, the cuisine of which also has some interesting barley dishes. These, as befits a region with a longer history and direct contact with the neighbouring Middle Eastern lands, are more spicy and generally richer. The one below is for a barley pilav with fresh coriander. If this is not available use chopped parsley instead. The taste will not be same, but it is still delicious.

Kintzov gari – pearl barley with fresh coriander

1.2l (2 pints) water
350g (12oz) pearl barley, rinsed thoroughly under cold water drained
1 teaspoon salt
50g (2oz) butter
1 green pepper, seeded and finely chopped
1 red pepper, seeded and finely chopped
1 teaspoon paprika
½ teaspoon chilli pepper
4 tablespoons finely chopped coriander

1 Bring the water to the boil in a large saucepan. Add the barley and salt and cover the pan. Lower the heat and simmer for about 45 minutes or until the water has been absorbed and the grains are tender.
2 Meanwhile melt the butter in a small pan, add the green and red peppers and fry for 2–3 minutes until they have softened.

Stir in the remaining ingredients and fry for a further 1–2
minutes.
3 Stir this mixture into the pilav, cover and set aside 'to rest'
for 5–10 minutes before serving.

Variation: Replace the red and green peppers with 1 large,
finely chopped onion; omit the coriander or parsley and use
1½ tablespoons dried basil instead.

Arpa şehriyesi domatesli – pearl barley with tomatoes

'Like barley, eaten but maligned.' – to be unfairly judged. *(Middle
Eastern expression)*

75g (3oz) butter
1 large onion, chopped
1 teaspoon cumin seeds
450g (1lb) tomatoes, blanched, peeled and chopped
350g (12oz) pearl barley, rinsed thoroughly under cold water and
    drained
3 cloves
2 tablespoons raisins
2 tablespoons slivered almonds
1 teaspoon salt
1.2l (2 pints) boiling water

1 Melt the butter in a large saucepan, add the onion and fry
until soft, stirring occasionally. Add the cumin seeds and
barley and fry for a further 3–4 minutes, stirring regularly.
2 Stir in the remaining ingredients and bring to the boil.
Reduce the heat to low, cover the pan and simmer for about
45–60 minutes or until the liquid has been absorbed and the
grains are tender. Stir occasionally.
3 Remove from the heat, leave to 'rest' for a few minutes and
then serve with salads, yoghurt and pickles OR as an
accompaniment to a meat dish.

Arpa ve kuru fasulya pilavi – barley and bean pilav

This simple and delicious dish from Anatolia is usually eaten
with bread and yoghurt, but also makes an ideal

accompaniment to any meat dish. It is also very tasty served
cold, as a salad!

225g (8oz) red kidney beans OR haricot beans, soaked in cold water
  overnight
110g (4oz) pearl barley, rinsed thoroughly under cold water and
  drained
3 tablespoons oil
2 medium onions, finely chopped
2 cloves garlic, finely chopped
1 teaspoon chilli pepper
1 teaspoon salt
3 tablespoons finely chopped parsley
½ teaspoon dillweed
1 tablespoon lemon juice

1 Drain and rinse the beans. Place them in a large saucepan
with plenty of cold water and bring to the boil. Cook rapidly for
10 minutes, then lower the heat and simmer for about 45–60
minutes or until just tender. Drain.
2 Meanwhile cook the barley in the same way and then drain.
3 While the beans and barley are cooking heat the oil in a
large saucepan, add the onion and garlic and fry until soft,
stirring frequently. Add the drained beans and barley and all
the remaining ingredients. Stir well and then set aside to 'rest'
for a few minutes before serving.

Ashe jo-ve-nokhod – pearl barley and chickpea casserole

'Our barley rather than another's wheat.' – *Egyptian saying*

This dish can either be cooked on the hob or in the oven. The
vegetables can vary according to availability and taste. The
two constant ingredients are barley and chickpeas which are
much used in Kurdistan – one of those geographical areas
which, although it has been around for nearly three millenia,
still does not exist politically.
  If you do not like your food too hot, cut down the quantity of
chilli pepper used. The Kurds would probably also munch fresh
green chillies while eating this dish!

50g (2oz) butter
1 large onion, thinly sliced
2 cloves garlic, finely chopped
175g (6oz) chickpeas, soaked in cold water overnight
225g (8oz) pearl barley, rinsed thoroughly under cold water and
    drained
1.2l (2 pints) boiling water
3 bay leaves
1 large carrot, halved lengthways and thinly sliced
1 large courgette, thinly sliced
1 teaspoon salt
½ teaspoon black pepper
1½ teaspoons chilli pepper
3 tablespoons finely chopped parsley or coriander
1 teaspoon dried basil

1 Heat the butter in a large saucepan or casserole and add the
onion and garlic. Fry until soft, stirring regularly. Drain and
rinse the chickpeas and add to the pan together with the
barley, water and bay leaves. Bring to the boil, reduce the heat
to low, cover the pan and cook for 30 minutes.
2 Add the carrot, courgette, salt, pepper and chilli pepper and
mix thoroughly. Cover the pan and cook for a further
40–45 minutes, stirring occasionally.
3 Remove from the heat and stir in the parsley or coriander
and basil before serving.

Ragoût de moutonà l'orge – mutton with barley

A French classic. Ragoûts are made with the shoulder, neck,
neck chops or breast of the sheep. However, you can use lamb
instead.
    Serve with bread or roast potatoes.

350g (12oz) pearl barley, rinsed thoroughly under cold water and
    drained
75g (3oz) butter or fat
675g (1½lb) mutton or lamb, cut into 2.5cm (1″) cubes
1 teaspoon salt
1 teaspoon black pepper

¼ teaspoon chilli pepper
2 cloves garlic, crushed
2 heaped tablespoons flour
600ml (1 pint) water or clear stock

1 Place the pearl barley in a saucepan, cover with plenty of lightly salted water and bring to the boil. Lower the heat and simmer for 30 minutes.
2 Meanwhile melt the butter or fat in a large saucepan and add the meat. Sauté for about 20 minutes, stirring frequently.
3 Season the meat with the salt, pepper, chilli pepper and garlic. Sprinkle in the flour and stir well. Add the water and bring to the boil, stirring constantly.
4 Drain the barley and stir it into the meat mixture. Reduce the heat to low, cover the pan and cook for a further 30–40 minutes, stirring occasionally, until the liquid has been absorbed.
5 Remove from the heat and serve.

Salen jawe – curried barley

A beautiful dish, full of 'eastern' flavour. Plantains (green bananas) can be bought from Indian and West Indian shops.
    Serve on its own or as an accompaniment to another curry or with a simple grilled or roasted meat dish.

'Long summer rains –
barley's as tasteless
as the sky.'
                    17th century. Mokusetsu (Penguin Book of Zen Poetry)

350g (12oz) pearl barley, rinsed thoroughly under cold water and
  drained
1.2l (2 pints) water
1 teaspoon salt
3 tablespoons mango chutney
50g (2oz) desiccated coconut
50g (2oz) raisins
50g (2oz) cashew nuts, toasted under the grill until golden
2 teaspoons curry powder
1 teaspoon garam masala

2 plantains, peeled and cut into 1cm (½″) slices then tossed in
  2 tablespoons lemon juice

1 Place the barley, water and salt in a pan and bring to the
boil. Reduce the heat to low, cover the pan and cook for 45–60
minutes or until the liquid has been absorbed.
2 Add all the remaining ingredients and mix thoroughly.
Cover and cook for a further 5–10 minutes, stirring gently once
or twice.
3 Remove from the heat and leave to 'rest' for a few minutes
before serving.

Barley, fruit and vegetable pollo

This is a really marvellous dish.

350g (12oz) pearl barley, washed thoroughly and drained
900ml (1½ pints) water
½ teaspoon salt
2 tablespoons tahina (see Glossary)
50g (2oz) butter
1 large onion, chopped
1 large green pepper, seeded and chopped
2 large carrots, peeled and diced
110g (4oz) peas
2 tablespoons finely chopped coriander or parsley
1 teaspoon salt
½ teaspoon black pepper
50g (2oz) raisins or sultanas
75g (3oz) dried apricots, coarsely chopped
50g (2oz) cashew nuts
2 tablespoons orange juice
1 tablespoon lemon juice
150ml (¼ pint) boiling water

1 Place the barley, water and ½ teaspoon salt in a saucepan
and bring to the boil. Lower the heat, cover the pan and cook
until the liquid has been absorbed and the grains are tender.
Remove from the heat and stir in the tahina.
2 Heat half the butter in a saucepan, add the onion and fry
until soft. Add the green pepper, carrots and peas and fry for a

further 3–4 minutes, stirring frequently. Stir in the coriander
or parsley, salt and pepper and set aside.
3 Melt the remaining butter in a small pan, add the raisins or
sultanas, apricots and cashew nuts and fry for 2–3 minutes.
Stir in the orange and lemon juice and set aside.
4 Generously grease a large ovenproof casserole and spread
half the barley over the bottom. Layer the vegetables over it
and then cover with half of the remaining barley. Spread the
fruit and nut mixture over it and then top with the rest of the
barley. Pour in the boiling water, fit the lid on tightly and
place in an oven preheated to 350°F, 180°C, Gas Mark 4. Bake
for 20–30 minutes and then remove and serve.

And finally this beguiling tale, with a moral, from the deserts
of Arabia. You need not fight your enemy, just kill his horses –
with barley, of course!

THE POISONED BARLEY
'Certain chronicles tell how a Sultan, besieged on all sides, devised
the following scheme to vanquish the foe. He took some barley, boiled
it in water with sprays of common oleander and put it out to dry. Then
he went with his soldiers to the advance posts and deposited the
barley in the nose-bags of the horses. When the enemy scouts
approached, he fled with his men, leaving the bags there.
   The enemy army followed the scouts and occupied the place. The
soldiers found the bags full of barley. They hung them round the
horses' necks. Shortly afterwards the fodder poisoned the horses and
they all fell lifeless to the ground. The Sultan then left the city with
his cavalry. He attacked the enemy troops and took them prisoner,
like a harvest ripe for the picking.'

                                                      The Subtle Ruse

Millet

*? Inca Wheat — Quinoa.
(Chenopodium quinoa)*

'He plants millet in front of the chicken.' – *Armenian saying*

The name 'millet' is applied to numerous small-seeded grasses
which originated in Africa and Asia. There are more than 400
species in the world, of which Common Millet (*Panicum*

*Chs family — like tea
Spinach !*

Miliaceum) is the most important one cultivated for grain. It is
a spring plant with a fibrous root system. It forms a shrub with
3–7 culms, 3 or 4 of which bear fruit which produce round, oval
or elongated grains, white, yellow or red in colour. The millet
found in shops is of this variety. There are others such as:
Setaria italica – foxtail millet, grown in China and India.
Papsalum Scorbiculatum – ditch millet, kodo
Eleusine Coracana – finger millet, birdsfoot millet, millet, ragi.
Grown in China and particularly Northern India where it
replaces rice as the principal cereal crop.
Proso millet is grown in the USSR and China.
Pearl millet is grown extensively in Africa and Asia. It is well
suited to conditions of limited moisture and low fertility.

The traditional method of preparation in Africa and Asia is
to pound the millet (or sorghum or teff) to loosen the husk and
reduce the grain to a wholemeal or semolina; then to winnow
it. The grains are stored and from it the day's requirements are
turned to flour or meal. From this, unleavened bread is
prepared. The wholemeal flour is cooked with water to make
porridge-type dishes and desserts. The whole grains are cooked
just like rice.

Millet is the oldest cultivated plant, known well over 12,000
years ago, but in the West the best we can do is give it to our
budgies!

The recipes below will illustrate how other nations and
cultures have made use of this excellent grain by creating
interesting dishes. The first one is a simple porridge-like dish
from Central Asia. It is traditionally prepared with *Proso*
grains, but any millet found in health food shops will do as
well.

Pshyenaya kasha s-maslom – millet and butter kasha

Serve as a porridge or with roast or grilled chicken.

1.2l (2 pints) water
1 teaspoon salt
50g (2oz) butter

250g (9oz) millet grains, washed thoroughly several times under cold
  water and drained

1 Place the water, salt and half the butter in a saucepan and
bring to the boil. Add the drained millet, reduce the heat to
low, cover the pan and cook for 30–40 minutes, stirring
occasionally, until the mixture is thick and porridge-like.
2 Just before serving stir in the remaining butter.

Variation 1: You can prepare this dish with milk. Bring 2.5l
(4 pints) milk to the boil, add the drained millet, lower the heat
and cook for 30 minutes. Stir in ½ teaspoon salt and 2
tablespoons sugar and cook for a further 30 minutes, stirring
occasionally.

Variation 2: Anan Geil – millet with honey
In this recipe the Somalis simply mix the millet into camel's
milk, stir in honey, cover and set aside for 1–2 hours before
serving as a savoury. You may find you have to substitute
cow's milk for the camel's milk!

110g (4oz) millet, washed very thoroughly under cold water and
  drained
600ml (1 pint) milk
60ml (2fl oz) 'runny' honey

1 Place all the ingredients in a bowl and mix until well
blended. Cover and refrigerate for 1–2 hours before serving.
  Serves 4.

Pshyenaya kasha s-teekvoy – millet kasha with pumpkin

This is a classic porridge-type dish which is often prepared
with milk instead of water.

1kg (2lb) pumpkin, peeled, seeded and cut into 2.5cm (1″) cubes
900ml (1½ pints) water
225g (8oz) millet, washed thoroughly under cold water and drained
50g (2oz) butter
150ml (¼ pint) single cream
1 teaspoon salt
½ teaspoon black pepper

¼ teaspoon nutmeg
1 teaspoon sugar

Garnish:
50g (2oz) melted butter (optional)

1 Place the pumpkin and water in a large saucepan and bring
to the boil. Lower the heat and simmer for 15 minutes.
2 Stir in the millet, cover the pan, reduce the heat as low as
possible and cook for 20 minutes.
3 Stir in all the remaining ingredients, re-cover the pan and
cook for a further 25–30 minutes, stirring occasionally.
4 To serve spoon the mixture into a large dish and, if you wish,
spoon over the extra melted butter.

Kroshit tchoomak s-greebom – millet and mushroom pilav,
Tchoomak-style

A Ukrainian speciality which makes a delicious savoury meal
in its own right.
   You can use extra bacon instead of the salt pork if you wish.

225g (8oz) millet, washed thoroughly under cold water and drained
450ml (¾ pint) water
110g (4 oz) salt pork (see page 228), cut into small pieces OR extra
   bacon
50g (2oz) bacon, cut into small pieces
1 large onion, coarsely chopped
675g (1½lb) button mushrooms, wiped clean and quartered
1 teaspoon salt

Garnish:
2 tablespoons finely chopped parsley, mint or tarragon

1 Place the millet and water in a large saucepan and bring to
the boil. Lower the heat, cover the pan and cook for 25 minutes.
2 Meanwhile fry the pieces of salt pork in a large frying pan
for a few minutes. (If using extra bacon, heat 2 tablespoons of
oil in the pan first, add all the bacon and fry for 2–3 minutes
before proceeding.) Add the bacon to the pork and fry for 2–3
minutes. Add the onion and fry until soft, stirring frequently.
Add the mushrooms and fry for 8–10 minutes, stirring
regularly.

3 After the millet has been cooking for 25 minutes stir the mushroom mixture into it.

4 Lightly grease an ovenproof dish and turn the millet pilav into it. Cover and cook in an oven preheated to 350°F, 180°C, Gas Mark 4 for 25–30 minutes. Garnish and serve immediately.

Holimar kita maash – Assyrian millet pilav

This very simple, but delicious pilav is popular throughout the Caucasus and Iran. Eat with fresh salad and yoghurt or serve as an accompaniment to roast and grilled meats.

75g (3oz) butter
350g (12oz) millet, washed thoroughly under cold water and drained
600ml (1 pint) water
1 teaspoon salt
½ teaspoon turmeric
1 teaspoon curry powder
1 large onion, coarsely chopped
50g (2oz) pistachio nuts, pine kernels or split almonds

Garnish:
2 tablespoons finely chopped parsley

1 Melt half the butter in a saucepan, add the millet and fry for a few minutes until the grains begin to turn golden. Add the water, salt, turmeric and curry powder and stir well. Bring to the boil, cover the pan, lower the heat and simmer for 25–30 minutes or until all the liquid has been absorbed.

2 Meanwhile melt the remaining butter in a small pan, add the onion and fry until soft. Add the nuts and fry, stirring frequently until they are golden.

3 When the millet has been cooking for 25–30 minutes stir in the onion and nut mixture, cover the pan and cook over a low heat for a further 5 minutes. Remove from the heat and leave to 'rest' for 5 minutes before serving.

Anadolu kazanli dari – Turkish millet casserole

A tasty, oven-baked pilav. You can vary the vegetables, depending on what you have or like.

Serve with a bowl of Shepherd's Salad (page 223), olives, pickles and yoghurt.

350g (12oz) millet, washed thoroughly under cold water and drained
450ml (¾ pint) water
1 teaspoon salt
4 tablespoons oil
1 large onion, chopped
2 cloves garlic, finely chopped
110g (4oz) haricot beans, soaked overnight in cold water, drained and
  cooked in boiling water until just tender
450g (1lb) tomatoes, blanched, peeled and chopped
2 courgettes, cut into 1cm (½″) slices
110g (4oz) mushrooms, wiped clean and sliced
2 medium carrots, peeled and thinly sliced
1 tablespoon dillweed
2 tablespoons finely chopped coriander or parsley
1 teaspoon salt
1 teaspoon chilli pepper

1 Place the millet, water and salt in a saucepan and bring to the boil. Lower the heat, cover the pan and simmer until all the liquid has been absorbed. Set aside.
2 Meanwhile heat the oil in a large saucepan, add the onion and garlic and fry until soft. Stir in all the remaining ingredients, cover the pan and cook over a low heat.
3 Stir the cooked millet into the vegetables.
4 Lightly grease an ovenproof casserole and turn the vegetable mixture into it. Cover and cook in an oven preheated to 350°F, 180°C, Gas Mark 4 for about 30 minutes. Remove and serve.

Garaw bil-fistuk – Palestinian millet pilav

Another delicious pilav full of flavour, colour and texture.
   Garaw is better known in English as *Aleppo millet grass* or *Cube grass*. It is a member of the *Gramineae* family. Since this grain is not available here, use the common millet.

350g (12oz) millet, washed thoroughly under cold water and drained
450ml (¾ pint) water

1 teaspoon salt
4 tablespoons oil
1 large onion, thinly sliced
2 small leeks, thinly sliced and washed thoroughly
1 stick celery, thinly sliced
2 medium carrots, peeled and diced
110g (4oz) mushrooms, wiped clean and sliced
2 tablespoons finely chopped tarragon, chives or coriander
1 teaspoon salt
½ teaspoon black pepper
50g (2oz) sultanas or raisins

Garnish:
yoghurt-garlic sauce (page 223) OR natural yoghurt

1 Place the millet, water and salt in a saucepan and bring to
the boil. Lower the heat, cover the pan and simmer until all the
water has been absorbed. Set aside.
2 Meanwhile heat the oil in a large saucepan, add the onion
and fry until soft. Stir in all the remaining ingredients, cover
the pan and cook for 15 minutes, stirring occasionally.
3 Stir in the cooked millet, cover the pan and cook for a further
15–20 minutes, stirring frequently. Serve with yoghurt –
garlic sauce or plain yoghurt.

Jero – millet with smoked fish

This is a Nigerian speciality. Often it is prepared with a local
grain called *Acha*, which is not available outside Africa, but
millet will do equally well.

Dry smoked fish is sold in Indian, Chinese and West Indian
shops.

This is a most unusual and tasty dish.

120ml (4fl oz) vegetable or groundnut oil
1 onion, thinly sliced
225g (8oz) minced meat
1 teaspoon salt
450g (1lb) tomatoes, blanched, peeled and chopped
600ml (1 pint) water
2 tablespoons tomato purée

1 teaspoon chilli pepper
450g (1lb) dry smoked fish, washed, boned and cut into smaller pieces
250g (9oz) millet, washed very thoroughly under cold water and
  drained

1 Heat half the oil in a large saucepan, add the onion and fry
until soft. Stir in the meat and salt and fry for 5–10 minutes,
stirring frequently.
2 Meanwhile heat the remaining oil in another pan, add the
tomatoes and fry for a few minutes. Stir in the water, tomato
purée and chilli pepper and bring to the boil. Lower the heat,
cover the pan and simmer for 10 minutes.
3 Pour the tomato mixture into the meat pan, add the fish and
mix well. Cover and cook for 5 minutes.
4 Stir in the millet, cover the pan and continue to simmer for
30–40 minutes or until the millet is tender. If the mixture
becomes too dry while cooking add a little more water.
5 Serve immediately.

Birabisko da taushe – millet with beef and vegetables

A favourite of West Africa. The jero (millet) is coarsely crushed
– you need not do this – and is served with a meat and
vegetable stew called 'taushe'.
  This is a rich and exotic dish.
  You can buy raw peanuts from most health food shops and
many supermarkets. Reduce them to a powder in a blender or
grinder.

50g (2oz) butter or ghee
350g (12oz) millet, washed very thoroughly under cold water and
  drained
450ml (¾ pint) water
1 teaspoon salt

Stew:
50g (2oz) butter
1 large onion, thinly sliced
450g (1lb) beef, cut into 2.5cm (1″) cubes
450g (1lb) tomatoes, blanched, peeled and cooked

1 teaspoon salt
1 teaspoon chilli pepper
450ml (¾ pint) water
450g (1lb) pumpkin flesh OR courgettes, cut into 4cm (1½″) pieces
450g (1lb) mixed vegetables of your choice e.g. sliced celery,
  cauliflower florets, sliced beans, chopped spinach, carrots etc.
110g (4oz) raw peanuts, finely ground

1 Melt the butter in a saucepan, add the millet and fry for a
few minutes until the grains are well coated and the butter has
been absorbed. Add the water and salt and bring to the boil.
Lower the heat, cover the pan and simmer for about 20
minutes. or until the liquid has been absorbed and the grains
are tender. Set aside.
2 To prepare the stew melt the butter in a large pan, add the
onion and fry until soft. Add the meat cubes and fry for 8–10
minutes, stirring frequently until evenly browned. Add the
tomatoes, salt, chilli pepper and water and bring to the boil.
Lower the heat, cover the pan and simmer for 30 minutes.
3 Add the pumpkin or courgettes and cook for 15 minutes and
then stir in the remaining vegetables and the ground peanuts.
Cover the pan and continue to cook over a low heat for 15–20
minutes, stirring occasionally, until the vegetables and meat
are tender.
4 To serve, heat the millet pilav through and then transfer it
to a large dish. Either make a well in the centre and pile the
'taushe' into it OR mix the stew and millet together. Serve
immediately.

Rye

Rye is a relatively new member of the cultivated cereal family.
It was unknown to the ancients (Egyptians, Sumerians,
Greeks). It only appeared in its present form in Europe in the
Middle Ages. Rye formed the basis of bread in most of medieval
Europe. Indeed, today Eastern Europe is the largest producer
and user of rye. One of the reasons is that rye tolerates the

extreme climate of Eastern Europe. The favourite Russian black bread is made from rye flour.

Rye does taste good, has a low gluten content and consequently will soon fill you up. You can use rye grains to make pilavs, although they take longer to cook and have a much 'chewier' texture than wheat or barley. Given below are two ways in which rye grains can be used, but you can experiment to your heart's content by varying the vegetables and meats used.

Rujanoy kasha – rye pilav

A typical kasha from Russia.

You can add to, or vary, the vegetables that I have used.

Serve with salads, pickles and soured cream. If you wish to serve it as an accompaniment to a meat dish then omit the cheese.

350g (12oz) rye grains, rinsed and soaked overnight in cold water
50g (2oz) butter
1 large onion, finely sliced
1 clove garlic, crushed
2 green peppers, seeded and thinly sliced
2 medium carrots, peeled and diced
2 sticks celery, thinly sliced
1 teaspoon salt
½ teaspoon black pepper
1 teaspoon paprika
1 teaspoon basil
300ml (½ pint) boiling water or stock
50g (2oz) grated cheese

Garnish:
2 tablespoons finely chopped tarragon or coriander

1 Drain the rye grains and place in a large saucepan. Cover well with water and bring to the boil. Lower the heat, cover the pan and simmer for about 1 hour. Add more boiling water if necessary. Drain.
2 Meanwhile melt the butter in a large saucepan, add the

onion and garlic and fry until soft. Add the remaining
vegetables and the seasonings and stir well. Fry over a low
heat for 5 minutes, stirring frequently and then set aside.
3 Stir the drained, cooked rye into the vegetable mixture and
add the boiling water or stock. Cover the pan, reduce the heat
to low and simmer for 20–30 minutes or until all the liquid has
evaporated.
4 Finally, stir in the cheese and cook for a further 5 minutes.
Remove from the heat and leave to 'rest' for a few minutes
before serving.

Rye and chicken casserole

A wholesome meal with the rye adding a nutty, chewy flavour
and texture to the dish.
   Serve with a bowl of yoghurt, or with any of the
yoghurt-based accompaniments (page 219) and with a salad of
your choice.

350g (12oz) rye grains, rinsed and soaked overnight in cold water
50g (2oz) butter
6 chicken pieces
1 large onion, finely chopped
2 sticks celery, thinly sliced
1 large red or green pepper, seeded and thinly sliced
1 teaspoon salt
1 teaspoon turmeric
1 teaspoon paprika
300ml (½ pint) boiling water or chicken stock
3 large tomatoes, blanched, peeled and thickly sliced
50g (2oz) raisins

Garnish:
A few green and black olives

1 Drain the rye and place in a large saucepan. Cover well with
water and bring to the boil. Lower the heat, cover the pan and
simmer for about 1 hour, adding more boiling water if
necessary. Drain.
2 Meanwhile melt the butter in a large, ovenproof casserole,

add the chicken pieces and fry for a few minutes, turning
frequently. Remove and reserve.
3 Add the onion to the butter and fry until soft, stirring
occasionally. Add the celery and pepper and fry for a further
2–3 minutes. Return the chicken pieces to the pan, season with
the salt, turmeric and paprika and mix well. Cover and cook in
an oven preheated to 350°F, 180°C, Gas Mark 4 for about 30
minutes.
4 Remove from the oven and arrange the drained rye over the
chicken and vegetables. Arrange the tomato slices over the
rye, add the boiling water or stock and cover the casserole.
Return to the oven and cook for a further 45 minutes. Ten
minutes before the end of the cooking time sprinkle the raisins
into the casserole.
5 Remove from the oven and serve.

Maize

The largest of the cereal plants, often reaching a height of over
3 metres (10ft). Originating in Mexico, it is now a major crop in
tropical and sub-tropical parts of the world. The grains of
maize ('corn' in Britain) grow in highly packed rows on an ear
(cob). Each plant produces 1 or 2 ripe ears, 15–20cm (6"–8")
long. There are many varieties. The main one is Dent corn
which is dried and ground into meal. The colour is white, but
there are variations – yellow, red, purple and black.

Use sweetcorn – the whole grain, fresh from a corn on the cob
or the frozen variety which is equally good.

Succotash – maize with meat

The American Indians cooked corn with beans in bear grease.
The early colonists added other ingredients such as meat and
spices. Below is an authentic recipe, but I suggest that you
might like to fry one chopped onion in a little butter before
adding the meat and then proceeding with the directions
below.

110g (4oz) red kidney beans, soaked overnight in cold water
450g (1lb) lean lamb or beef, cut into 1cm (½″) pieces
600ml (1 pint) water
450g (1lb) sweetcorn kernels
1 teaspoon salt
¾ teaspoon chilli pepper
2 tablespoons flour

1 Drain the kidney beans, place in a saucepan, cover well with
water and bring to the boil. Cook rapidly for 10 minutes, then
lower the heat and simmer for 45–60 minutes or until the
beans are just tender. Drain.
2 Place the meat in a saucepan with the water and bring to the
boil. Remove any scum that appears on the surface. Add the
sweetcorn, cover the pan and simmer for 20–30 minutes.
3 Stir in the beans, salt, pepper and flour, cover and simmer
for a further 10–15 minutes or until the meat is tender. Add a
little more water if the stew is too dry for your taste.
4 Serve with bread and salad.

Irio – maize with plantain

This maize-based dish from Kenya is delicious. Traditionally it
is mashed before serving, but I suggest you leave the
vegetables whole and serve them with the meat sauce below.

350g (12oz) sweetcorn kernels
750ml (1¼ pints) water
2 large plantains peeled and cut into 5cm (2″) pieces
675g (1½lb) potatoes, peeled and cut into 4cm (1½″) pieces
225g (8oz) peas
50g (2oz) butter
1 teaspoon salt

Meat sauce:
1 tablespoon butter
450g (1lb) lean lamb or beef, cut into 1cm (½″) pieces
1 onion, thinly sliced
225g (½lb) tomatoes, blanched, peeled and chopped
150ml (¼ pint) water
1 teaspoon tomato purée

1 teaspoon salt
½ teaspoon black pepper
½ teaspoon dillweed
½ teaspoon chilli pepper

1 Place the sweetcorn in a large saucepan with the water and
bring to the boil. Lower the heat, cover the pan and simmer for
15 minutes.
2 Add the plantains, potatoes and peas, cover the pan and
continue to cook until the vegetables are tender and the water
evaporated.
3 Stir in the butter and salt, cover and cook for a further 5–10
minutes, stirring occasionally.
4 You can now either mash the vegetables or serve them as
they are with the meat sauce.
5 Meanwhile to prepare the meat sauce, melt the butter in a
pan, add the pieces of meat and fry for 4–5 minutes, stirring
regularly. Add the onion and fry for a further 3–4 minutes.
5 Stir in all the remaining ingredients, cover the pan and cook
over a low heat, stirring frequently, for 30–40 minutes or until
the meat is tender.
6 To serve, spoon some of the meat sauce over the corn
mixture.

Egbo – maize with pepper sauce

With this popular Nigerian dish the cooked sweetcorn is served
with a pepper sauce.
   You can, as with the recipe above, either mash the maize or,
as I prefer, serve the kernels whole.
   A tasty, simple dish.

450g (1lb) sweetcorn kernels

Pepper sauce:
120ml (4fl oz) palm nut or peanut oil
1 large onion, finely chopped
2 green peppers, seeded and finely chopped
225g (8oz) tomatoes, blanched, peeled and chopped
1 teaspoon salt

1 teaspoon chilli pepper
2–3 spring onions, thinly sliced

1 Place the sweetcorn in a large saucepan and cover well with water. Bring to the boil, lower the heat and simmer for 10–15 minutes or until tender. Drain.
2 Meanwhile prepare the sauce by heating the oil in a saucepan. Add the onion and fry for a few minutes until soft. Add the green peppers and fry for a further 2–3 minutes. Stir in all the remaining ingredients, cover the pan and cook for 12–15 minutes, stirring occasionally.
3 Serve by spooning the sauce over the kernels.

Dara misri bil spanikh – maize with spinach

An Egyptian speciality. Maize (Dara) was introduced into Egypt (late 17th century) whence it travelled into the other Middle-Eastern lands – hence the name. 'Corn of Egypt' [Dara misri].

110g (4oz) chickpeas, soaked overnight in cold water
350g (12oz) sweetcorn kernels
600ml (1 pint) water
675g (1½lb) fresh spinach, all coarse stems and leaves discarded, washed very thoroughly and chopped finely
4 tablespoons oil
1 large onion, coarsely chopped
225g (½lb) tomatoes, blanched, peeled and chopped
350ml (¾ pint) water
Juice 1 lemon
1 teaspoon salt
½ teaspoon cumin
½ teaspoon chilli pepper
8–10 black olives, stoned and thinly sliced

1 Drain the chickpeas and place in a saucepan. Cover well with water and bring to the boil. Lower the heat and simmer for 45–60 minutes or until tender. Add more boiling water if necessary. Drain.
2 Place the sweetcorn in a saucepan with the water and bring

to the boil. Lower the heat and simmer for 10 minutes. Add the spinach and cooked chickpeas and stir well. Simmer for a further 5–8 minutes and then strain into a colander and leave to drain.

3 Meanwhile heat the oil in a large pan, add the onion and fry until soft. Add all the remaining ingredients and simmer for about 10 minutes or until the mixture thickens.

4 .Stir the corn and spinach mixture into the sauce, simmer for a few minutes and serve.

Grain Salads

'My Majesty made for him a garden
a new in order to present to him
vegetables and all beautiful flowers.' (offerings of Shutmose III to
Amon Ra) – *ancient records of Egypt*

The ancients were well aware of the many faceted qualities of
grains. They not only baked bread with them, cooked them in
stews and gruels and made desserts with them, but also, and
equally important, mixed them with vegetables and herbs to
make pilavs served warm and salads served cold.

In this chapter we have several grain salads. They are all
simple to prepare, economical and often very attractive in
appearance. They make excellent buffet fare and are also ideal
as a lunch or to accompany meat dishes. The ancient
Egyptians, Sumerians and Hittites had no rice. They used
wheat, cracked wheat, sorghum, millet and barley. Hence the
first few recipes in this chapter are salads prepared with these
grains.

The classic *tabouleh* from Syria probably dates back to those
early centuries of Mediterranean culinary history. Today it is
eaten as a salad in its own right, or as part of a larger *Mezzeh*
table.

Tabouleh – burghul and vegetable salad

150g (5oz) fine burghul
1 cucumber, finely chopped
6 tomatoes, finely chopped
2 green peppers, seeded and finely chopped
1 onion, finely chopped
6 tablespoons finely chopped parsley
3 tablespoons dried mint
1½ teaspoons salt
Juice 3–4 lemons
6 tablespoons olive oil

To serve:
1 lettuce, preferably Cos, leaves separated and washed

1 Rinse the burghul in a bowl several times until the water
runs clean. Squeeze out any excess water.

2 Put the chopped vegetables, parsley and mint into a large mixing bowl and add the burghul. Stir in the salt, lemon juice and oil. Mix well and leave for 15 minutes. Then taste and adjust the seasoning if necessary.

3 Arrange the lettuce leaves around the edge of a serving plate and pile the salad into the centre.

The traditional way of eating this salad is to make a parcel of the tabouleh by folding a little of it up in a lettuce leaf, or spooning a little of it into the 'pouch' of a pita bread.

Bazerghen – burghul and walnut salad

Again from Syria, and no doubt of Assyrian heritage, this refreshing salad has an earthy taste.

Serve with lettuce leaves, olives and sliced radishes.

175g (6oz) fine burghul
6 tablespoons olive oil
1 onion, finely chopped
1 teaspoon oregano
4 tablespoons finely chopped parsley
3 tablespoons walnuts, finely chopped
¾ teaspoon coriander
¾ teaspoon allspice
1½ teaspoons salt
¾ teaspoon black pepper
¾ teaspoon cayenne pepper
3 tablespoons tomato purée dissolved in 3–4 tablespoons water

1 Place the burghul in a bowl and rinse several times with cold water until the water runs clear. Soak the burghul in water for 5 minutes and then drain and squeeze out any excess water.

2 Meanwhile heat the oil in a small pan and fry the onion until soft and transparent.

3 Place the burghul in a large bowl and add the onion and oil. Add all the remaining ingredients and mix thoroughly. Place in the refrigerator to chill until ready to serve.

Each – Armenian burghul salad

Not to be outdone, and to show that culinary culture is always older than nations and languages, this Armenian salad from Southern Turkey is also popular with the Kurds, Arabs and Turks of the region.

Serve with pita bread and/or lettuce leaves.

175g (6oz) fine burghul
6 tablespoons finely chopped parsley
1 large onion, finely chopped
3 spring onions, finely chopped
3 large tomatoes, finely chopped
1 teaspoon salt
¾ teaspoon cumin
¾ teaspoon cayenne pepper
1½ tablespoons tomato purée
2 tablespoons pomegranate syrup OR 4 tablespoons lemon juice
5–6 tablespoons olive oil

1 Rinse the burghul in a large bowl and squeeze out excess moisture. Add all the remaining ingredients and mix well. Set aside for 15 minutes and then taste and adjust seasoning if necessary.
2 Pile the salad into a serving dish and eat with lettuce leaves and pita bread.

Tzavari aghtsan – Caucasian burghul salad

'In summer eat grapes, in winter sugar-cane.' – *Egyptian saying*

225g (8oz) fine burghul
1 stick celery, trimmed and thinly sliced
1 carrot, peeled and grated
50g (2oz) raisins or sultanas
110g (4oz) black or white grapes, halved and pipped
25g (1oz) slivered almonds, toasted until golden under the grill

Dressing:
4 tablespoons oil
3 tablespoons lemon juice
1 teaspoon salt

½ teaspoon allspice
½ teaspoon basil
2 tablespoons brandy
2 tablespoons tahina (see page 00)

Garnish:
2 tablespoons chopped tarragon or coriander

1   Place the burghul in a bowl and rinse with cold water until
the water runs clean. Soak the burghul in water for 5 minutes
and then drain and squeeze out any excess moisture.
2   Mix the burghul and remaining salad ingredients together
in a large bowl and set aside while you prepare the dressing.
3   Mix all the dressing ingredients together thoroughly in a
small bowl and pour them over the salad. Mix well and chill
until ready to serve.

Tsawar ba mast – burghul and yoghurt salad

From Kurdistan, two of the main ingredients of the region –
burghul and yoghurt – are combined with vegetables to create
an interesting salad.

A local garlic (Musir), a cross between onion and garlic, is
unfortunately unavailable outside the region, so I have
compromised by including garlic and onion as substitutes.
However, you can also use two shallots. In which case omit the
onion and garlic.

225g (8oz) fine burghul
¼ red cabbage, finely shredded
1 small onion, finely chopped
1 clove garlic, crushed
2–3 green chillis, thinly sliced
50g (2oz) hazelnuts, coarsely chopped
2 teaspoons sesame seeds, toasted until golden under the grill
1 large carrot, peeled and grated

Dressing:
300ml (½ pint) yoghurt
1 teaspoon salt
½ teaspoon dried mint
½ teaspoon dried dillweed

Garnish:
2 tablespoons finely chopped coriander or tarragon

1 Place the burghul in a bowl and rinse until the water runs clear. Soak the burghul in cold water for 5 minutes and then drain and squeeze out excess moisture.
2 Place the burghul in a large bowl and add all the salad ingredients. Stir well and set aside.
3 Mix all the dressing ingredients together and pour over the salad. Stir well and refrigerate until ready to serve.

Kharn hadgi aghtsan – mixed grain salad

'I'll make of your life a carob, black and twisted.'
– *Egyptian expression*

In this salad, wholewheat, burghul and rye are mixed together with carob juice (pekmez). In Turkey pekmez is made with grape juice. If carob juice is unobtainable you can use thick syrup or, better still, honey.

The combination of grains do vary. You can use pearl barley and/or buckwheat if you wish.

An unusual and delicious salad.

110g (4oz) rye or barley, washed and soaked overnight in cold water
50g (2oz) wholewheat grains, washed and soaked overnight in cold water
50g (2oz) chickpeas, washed and soaked overnight in cold water
110g (4oz) large burghul, rinsed in cold water
Juice 1 large lemon
3 tablespoons carob juice or honey
3 tablespoons finely chopped tarragon, coriander or parsley
1 teaspoon salt
1 teaspoon paprika
½ teaspoon marjoram or dillweed
2 tablespoons oil
1 onion, thinly sliced
1 clove garlic, crushed
1 stick celery, thinly sliced
½ teaspoon cinnamon
1 tablespoon raisins

2 tablespoons chopped nuts (almonds, pistachios or pine kernels),
 optional

1 Drain the rye, wholewheat and chickpeas and cook each
separately in pans of simmering water until tender. The rye
and wholewheat should take 30–45 minutes, but the chickpeas
will take longer. When tender drain them and rinse under cold
water.
2 Place the burghul in a bowl and rinse until the water runs
clear. Soak it in cold water for 10 minutes and then drain and
squeeze out excess moisture.
3 Pláce the burghul in a large bowl and stir in the cooked
grains and chickpeas.
4 In a small bowl mix together the lemon juice, carob juice or
honey, tarragon, salt, paprika and marjoram. Reserve.
5 Heat the oil in a small pan, add the onion and fry until soft.
Stir in the garlic, celery, cinnamon, raisins and nuts and fry for
3–4 minutes, stirring frequently.
6 Add the lemon juice dressing and the fried vegetable
mixture to the grain salad and mix thoroughly. Refrigerate for
a while and then serve.

Daroni aghtsan – chicken and barley salad

A family recipe. The chicken can be substituted with other
cooked meat.

225g (8oz) pearl barley, washed thoroughly and drained
1kg (2lb) cooked chicken flesh, cut into 1cm (½″) cubes
1 onion, finely chopped
1 green pepper, seeded and thinly sliced
½ cucumber, peeled and chopped
6 radishes, thinly sliced
1 large carrot, peeled and grated

Dressing:
Juice 1 lemon
1 tablespoon pomegranate syrup diluted in 3 tablespoons water OR
2 more tablespoons lemon juice
4 tablespoons oil
1 teaspoon salt

Garnish:
2 tablespoons chopped pistachio nuts

1 Place the pearl barley in a bowl, cover with water and leave
to soak for 1 hour.
2 Drain it and place in a saucepan. Cover with water and
bring to the boil. Lower the heat and simmer for 30–45
minutes, or until tender. Drain.
3 Place the barley in a large bowl and stir in all the remaining
salad ingredients.
4 Mix the dressing ingredients together in a small bowl and
pour over the salad. Stir well and refrigerate for 1 hour.
Garnish and serve.

Green rice salad

A lovely 'greenish' salad from Italy which is extremely
attractive when moulded into a ring.
    Serve with cold or grilled meats and kebabs.

225g (8oz) Italian *Avouo* or long-grain rice, washed thoroughly and
  drained
450ml (¾ pint) water
1 teaspoon salt
225g (8oz) fresh spinach, stalks and coarse leaves discarded, washed
  very thoroughly
110g (4oz) peas, cooked

Dressing:
3 tablespoons oil
1 tablespoon lemon juice
1 level teaspoon salt
½ teaspoon black pepper
½ teaspoon sugar
½ teaspoon basil
½ teaspoon marjoram

1 Place the rice in a saucepan with the water and salt and
bring to the boil. Lower the heat, cover the pan and simmer
until all the liquid has been absorbed.
2 Meanwhile half fill a large pan with lightly salted water and

bring to the boil. Chop the spinach coarsely, add to the boiling water and simmer for 5–7 minutes. Drain into a colander and press it down with a wooden spoon to extract excess moisture. Chop the spinach very finely.

3 When cooked turn the rice into a large bowl and mix in the spinach and peas.

4 Mix the dressing ingredients together in a small bowl and pour it over the salad. Mix thoroughly.

5 Lightly grease a 1.2l (2 pint) ring mould and spoon the salad into it. Press the salad down and smooth over the surface. Refrigerate for at least 1 hour.

6 To serve place a large plate over the mould and then invert. If you wish the ring can be garnished with sprigs of watercress and radish slices.

Rice and beetroot salad

A colourful and tasty salad which is excellent on a buffet table.

350g (12oz) long-grain rice, washed thoroughly under cold water and
  drained
720ml (24fl oz) boiling water
1 teaspoon salt
1 large eating apple, peeled, cored and diced
1 teaspoon lemon juice
2 sticks celery, chopped
120ml (4fl oz) mayonnaise
3 tablespoons olive oil
1 tablespoon lemon juice
1 teaspoon salt
½ teaspoon black pepper
¼ teaspoon dry mustard
350g (12oz) cooked beetroot, peeled and diced
3 spring onions, trimmed and sliced
2 tablespoons finely chopped tarragon or parsley

Garnish:
Chopped parsley or tarragon

1 Place the rice in a saucepan with the boiling water and salt and boil vigorously for 1 minute. Lower the heat, cover the pan

and simmer for 15–20 minutes or until all the liquid has been absorbed. Remove from the heat and leave 'to rest'.

2 Place the diced apple in a large bowl and sprinkle with the lemon juice. Add the celery and mayonnaise and mix well.

3 Fluff up the rice with a long-pronged fork and stir into the mayonnaise mixture.

4 Place the oil, lemon juice, salt, pepper and mustard in a bowl and beat until well blended. Add the diced beetroot and spring onions and stir until well coated with the dressing.

5 Add this mixture to the rice, sprinkle in the parsley or tarragon and stir thoroughly. Refrigerate for 1–2 hours.

6 Transfer to a large serving bowl, garnish and serve.

Apricot and peach salad

A colourful and delicious salad which is ideal with roasts, especially pork and chicken, and with cold meats. Also good as a meal in its own right.

You can use fresh fruit or fruit preserved in natural juices.

250g (9oz) long-grain rice, washed thoroughly under cold water and
  drained
600ml (1 pint) boiling water
1 teaspoon salt
2 tablespoons oil
1 tablespoon lemon juice
1 tablespoon honey
6 tablespoons natural yoghurt
225g (8oz) peaches, blanched, peeled and thickly sliced
225g (8oz) apricots, blanched, peeled and quartered
225g (8oz) cooked ham, thinly sliced
2 sticks celery, thinly sliced
3 tablespoons slivered almonds, toasted under the grill until golden

1 Place the rice, water and salt in a saucepan and boil vigorously for 1 minute. Lower the heat, cover the pan and simmer for 15–20 minutes or until all the liquid has been absorbed. Set aside 'to rest'.

2 Place the oil, lemon juice, honey and yoghurt in a large bowl

and beat thoroughly. Stir in the peaches, apricots, ham, celery
and almonds.

3 Fluff up the rice with a long-pronged fork and mix into the
fruit. Refrigerate until ready to serve and then turn into a
large dish.

American fruit and nut salad

An absolutely brilliant salad which is marvellous on the buffet
table. Delicious on its own, but even better with cold meats.

   The fruit content can vary according to seasonal availability.

1 tablespoon butter
250g (9oz) long-grain rice, washed thoroughly under cold water and
   drained
600ml (1 pint) boiling water
1 teaspoon salt
3 tablespoons oil
2 oranges, peeled and segmented
350g (12oz) pineapple chunks, fresh or tinned in natural juices and
   drained
½ a medium honeydew or ogen melon, peeled and cut into 2.5cm (1″)
   cubes, or formed into small balls with a scoop
12–15 strawberries, sliced
12 olives
2 tablespoons chopped pistachio nuts
2 tablespoons pine kernels
12–15 small pickled gherkins

Dressing:
75g (3oz) brown sugar
4 tablespoons wine vinegar
1 teaspoon dry mustard
90ml (3fl oz) oil
2 tablespoons finely chopped tarragon OR 2 teaspoons dried tarragon
1 teaspoon sumac powder

Garnish:

Crisp lettuce leaves

1 Melt the butter in a saucepan, add the rice and fry for

2–3 minutes. Stir in the water and salt and boil vigorously for
1 minute. Lower the heat, cover the pan and simmer for 15–20
minutes or until all the liquid has been absorbed.
2 Turn the rice into a large bowl, toss in the 3 tablespoons of
oil and refrigerate when cool enough.
3 Mix all the salad ingredients together and stir into the rice.
4 Place all the dressing ingredients into a bowl and beat
thoroughly. Pour it over the salad and toss carefully.
5 Arrange the lettuce leaves on a large serving dish, pile the
salad into the centre and serve.

Ham and rice salad

A refreshing and tasty salad which makes a meal in itself or
can be served with grilled or cold meats.

350g (12oz) long-grain rice, washed thoroughly under cold water and
    drained
1 teaspoon salt
720ml (24fl oz) boiling water
225g (8oz) thick, cooked ham, cut into 1cm (½″) pieces
175g (6oz) pineapple, fresh or tinned, cut into small pieces
1 large red pepper, seeded and cut into 1cm (½″) squares
1 large eating apple, peeled, cored and chopped
50g (2oz) black olives

Dressing:
2 egg yolks
½ teaspoon salt
½ teaspoon dry mustard
75ml (2½fl oz) oil
Juice 1 small lemon
90ml (3fl oz) yoghurt
1 teaspoon paprika
1 tablespoon chopped fresh mint OR 1 teaspoon dried mint

Garnish:
Lettuce leaves
3–4 spring onions, thinly sliced

1 Place the rice, salt and water in a saucepan and boil
vigorously for 1 minute. Lower the heat, cover the pan, and

simmer for 15–20 minutes or until all the liquid has been absorbed. Set aside to cool.

2 Mix all the salad ingredients together in a large bowl. Fluff up the rice with a long-pronged fork and stir into the salad.

3 Place all the dressing ingredients in a bowl and whisk until well blended. Pour over the salad and toss thoroughly. Refrigerate.

4 Serve on a bed of lettuce leaves and sprinkle with the sliced spring onions.

Lobster salad

Lobster, rice, pineapple and prawns are mixed with a tasty mayonnaise to make an exquisite meal.

250g (9oz) long-grain rice, washed thoroughly under cold water and
  drained
1 teaspoon salt
600ml (1 pint) boiling water
2 × 675g (1½lb) cooked lobsters, shells split, claws cracked and grey
  sac removed
225g (8oz) prawns, peeled
225g (8oz) pineapple, fresh or tinned, cut into small chunks
1 green pepper, seeded and thinly sliced
6 large radishes, washed and thinly sliced
1 teaspoon salt
½ teaspoon black pepper

Mayonnaise:
2 egg yolks
⅛ teaspoon tabasco sauce
½ teaspoon salt
¼ teaspoon black pepper
2 teaspoons paprika
240ml (8fl oz) olive oil
2 tablespoons lemon juice
90ml (3fl oz) double cream, lightly whipped

Garnish:
lettuce leaves
4 hard-boiled eggs, sliced

4 tomatoes, thinly sliced
1 tablespoon finely chopped chives

1 Place the rice, salt and water in a saucepan and boil
vigorously for 1 minute. Lower the heat, cover the pan and
simmer for 15–20 minutes or until all the liquid has been
absorbed. Set aside to cool.
2 Prepare the mayonnaise by placing the egg yolks in a
medium-sized bowl. Add the tabasco, salt, pepper and paprika.
Using a wire whisk, beat the ingredients together. Add the oil,
a few drops at a time, whisking constantly. Do not add too
quickly or the mayonnaise will curdle. Beat in a few drops of
the lemon juice from time to time to prevent the mayonnaise
from becoming too thick. When all the oil has been added stir
in the remaining lemon juice and the cream. Taste for
seasoning and adjust if necessary. Set aside.
3 Remove the lobster meat from the shells and claws and chop
the meat into 2.5cm (1″) pieces. Place in a large bowl and add
the prawns, pineapple, green pepper, radishes, salt and pepper.
4 Fluff up the rice with a long-pronged fork and add to the
salad. Pour in the mayonnaise and toss well. Refrigerate until
ready to serve.
5 Line a large serving dish with lettuce leaves and arrange
the egg and tomato slices decoratively around the edge of the
dish. Spoon the lobster mixture into the centre and sprinkle
with the chives.

Fruits de mer en salade – seafood salad

A rich dish which is eye-catching and mouth-watering.
   Serve with bread and a green salad.

250g (9oz) long-grain rice, washed thoroughly under cold water and
   drained
1 teaspoon salt
1 teaspoon turmeric
600ml (1 pint) boiling water
350g (12oz) haddock, cod or halibut
½ onion, quartered

1 carrot, peeled and quartered
bay leaf
1 green pepper, seeded and diced
1 red pepper, seeded and diced
2 sticks celery, thinly sliced
50g (2oz) black olives, halved and stoned
175g (6oz) jar mussels
175g (6oz) prawns, peeled
110g (4oz) white crab meat

Dressing:
5 tablespoons oil
2 tablespoons lemon juice
1 large clove garlic, crushed
1 teaspoon salt
½ teaspoon black pepper

Garnish:
Lemon wedges

1 Place the rice, salt, turmeric and water in a saucepan and boil vigorously for 1 minute. Lower the heat, cover the pan and simmer for 15–20 minutes or until all the liquid is absorbed. Set aside to cool.

2 Meanwhile place the haddock, cod or halibut in a pan with the onion, carrot and bay leaf. Add enough lightly salted water to cover and poach the fish until it is tender. Remove the fish, discard the bones and skin and divide the flesh into bite-sized pieces.

3 Fluff up the rice with a long-pronged fork and turn into a large bowl. Add the vegetables, olives and all the fish. Mix together gently.

4 Place the dressing ingredients together in a bowl and whisk together. Pour over the salad and stir through gently. Refrigerate before serving with the lemon wedges.

Chirashi-zushi – Japanese rice and vegetable salad

'Fly dare take
the rice grain
on my chin.' – Rantsetsu *(Penguin Book of Zen Poetry)*

One of the very few cold rice salads from Japan. It is colourful, appetising and simple to prepare.

Vegetables can vary according to availability and most can be obtained from Chinese shops, and some large supermarkets.

Sushi rice:
350g (12oz) short-grain rice, washed thoroughly under cold water and
  drained
450ml (¾ pint) water
4 tablespoons rice vinegar or white vinegar
3 tablespoons sugar
2 teaspoons salt
2 tablespoons mirin OR dry sherry

Salad:
3–4 dried mushrooms, soaked in boiling water for 30 minutes
1 tablespoon soy sauce
1 teaspoon sugar
110g (4oz) prawns, peeled
1 tablespoon oil
2 eggs
¼ teaspoon salt
110g (4oz) finely sliced raw fish, e.g. Dover sole, lemon sole, tuna
  (optional)
75g (3oz) cooked peas
1 piece tinned lotus root, sliced
75g (3oz) finely sliced bamboo shoot
1 small white radish, thinly sliced
1 teaspoon grated fresh ginger

1 Place the rice in a saucepan with the water and bring to the boil. Lower the heat, cover and simmer for 15 minutes or until all the liquid has been absorbed. Set aside to cool.
2 In a large bowl mix the vinegar, sugar, salt and mirin together. Add the rice and stir thoroughly.
3 Drain the mushrooms and discard the stems. Slice the caps thinly and place in a saucepan with 120ml (4fl oz) water. Bring to the boil and simmer for 10 minutes. Add the soy sauce and sugar, cook for a further 2–3 minutes and set aside.
4 Place the prawns in a pan with a little water and simmer for 5 minutes. Drain and reserve.

5 Heat the oil in a frying pan. Place the eggs in a small bowl
with the salt and beat well. Pour into the pan and leave to cook
over a low heat until set. Remove from the pan, roll up and
then cut into thin strips.

6 Fluff up the rice with a long-pronged fork and place in a
large bowl. Add the mushrooms with their liquid, prawns, fish,
omelette strips, peas, vegetables and ginger and toss well.
Refrigerate until ready to serve.

Accompaniments

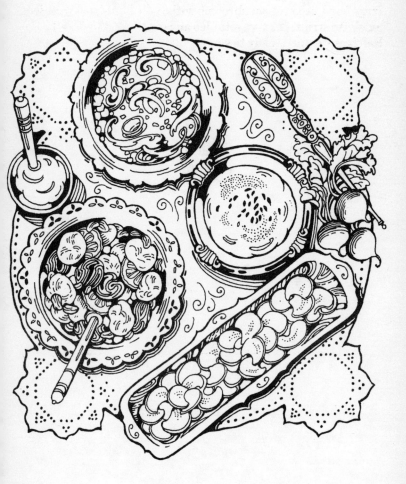

Dhunia chutney – coriander chutney

There are many variations of this chutney which is based on coriander leaves. Below is the basic one which you can vary with the addition of other vegetables, herbs and spices.

Dhunia chutney is excellent with all pilav dishes.

3 whole peppercorns
2 cloves garlic
2 green chillis OR 1 level tablespoon cayenne pepper
1 bunch fresh coriander leaves, rinsed thoroughly
½ teaspoon ground cumin
¼ teaspoon salt
Juice 1 lemon

1 Blend all the ingredients together with a mortar and pestle or in a liquidiser.
2 Transfer to a serving bowl and use sparingly.

Variations:
Try adding any of the following to the above ingredients.
a) 1 teaspoon mint
b) 1 tablespoon desiccated coconut
c) 2–3 tablespoons ground nuts of your choice
d) 2 tomatoes, blanched and peeled
e) 1 large cooked and mashed potato plus a little more lemon juice.

Raita – Indian yoghurt salad

This version of the Indian yoghurt salad is made with bananas.
It goes particularly well with spicy pilavs.

1 tablespoon oil
½ teaspoon mustard seeds
2 tablespoons desiccated coconut
600ml (1 pint) yoghurt
½ teaspoon salt
2 teaspoons dhunia chutney (see above)
1 large banana, thinly sliced

1 Heat the oil in a pan, add the mustard seeds and fry for

30 seconds. Stir in the coconut and remove from the heat.
2 Add a little of the yoghurt, the salt and chutney and mix
thoroughly. Add the remaining yoghurt and the banana slices
and stir gently. Transfer to a bowl and serve.

Khuri – yoghurt sauce

This is a yoghurt sauce which should accompany any of the
khitchri (kedgeree) dishes. However there is no reason why
you cannot serve it with any other rice pilav.

4 tablespoons coriander leaves, finely chopped
1 tablespoon desiccated coconut
2 cloves garlic
2 green chillis, chopped
1 tablespoon chopped onion
½ teaspoon salt
450ml (¾ pint) yoghurt
1 tablespoon gram flour (see Glossary) or plain flour
¼ teaspoon turmeric
2 tablespoons ghee
1 small onion, finely chopped
½ teaspoon whole cumin seeds

Garnish:
½ teaspoon dried mint or dried, crushed curry leaves
½ teaspoon paprika

1 With a mortar and pestle pound together the coriander
leaves, coconut, garlic, chillis, chopped onion and salt. When
smooth transfer to a saucepan and stir in the yoghurt, flour
and turmeric until smooth.
2 Place the pan over a low heat and cook, stirring constantly
until the mixture begins to simmer. Remove from the heat.
3 Meanwhile melt the ghee in a small pan and fry the onion
until soft. Remove the onion from the pan with a slotted spoon
and transfer to the yoghurt.
4 Add the whole cumin seeds and fry until they blacken.
Remove and add to the yoghurt pan.
5 Return the yoghurt pan to the heat and continue to cook

over a low heat, stirring constantly, until the mixture has the consistency of thin cream. Transfer to a bowl, garnish and serve.

Selada sumatera – Indonesian salad

This 'salad', really a meal in its own right, is what a good Indonesian will serve you with your bowl of rice. I suggest you do the same. It goes particularly well with plain pilavs and those with vegetables and fruits.

You can vary the proportions depending on the richness of the pilav.

¼ medium cabbage, cored and thinly sliced
110g (4oz) french beans, stringed and cut into 5cm (2″) pieces
110g (4oz) beansprouts

Sauce:
110g (4oz) peanuts, fried in 1 tablespoon oil and then finely chopped
2 green chillis, finely chopped
1 tablespoon lemon juice
1 teaspoon brown sugar
½ teaspoon salt
2–3 tablespoons lukewarm water

Omelette:
1 large egg, lightly beaten with ½ teaspoon salt and ¼ teaspoon black pepper
1 tablespoon water
1 tablespoon oil
1 large onion, chopped
½ cucumber, peeled, quartered and thinly sliced
1 large potato, boiled, peeled and coarsely chopped

1 Place the cabbage, french beans and beansprouts in the top of a steamer and set over boiling water. Steam for about 5 minutes, or until the vegetables are cooked, but still crisp. Remove from the heat and set aside.
2 Meanwhile prepare the sauce by mixing all the ingredients together. The final result should be a thick, but smooth sauce. Set aside.

3 Brush a small frying pan sparingly with oil. Beat the seasoned egg with the water and pour into the pan. Cook over a moderate heat until set. Slide out of the pan, roll up and cut into thin strips.
4 Heat the oil in the pan, add the onion and fry, stirring regularly, until crisp.
5 Place the steamed vegetables in a large bowl with the cucumber and potato. Add the sauce and mix thoroughly. Transfer to a serving dish and garnish with the omelette strips and fried onion.

Pisang goreng – fried bananas

Fried bananas are often served as an accompaniment to rice pilavs. The bananas can be ripe, but must be firm otherwise they will disintegrate.

3 large, or 6 medium, bananas, peeled
oil for frying
pinch salt

1 If using large bananas first cut them in half crossways.
2 Halve the bananas lengthways.
3 Heat a little oil in a large frying pan over a moderate heat. Add the banana pieces and fry, turning regularly, until evenly golden.
4 Remove carefully to a serving dish, sprinkle with a little salt and serve.

Ipekere – banana chips

'When there is no more wheat, barley, rice, sorghum or millet, we'll eat bananas.' – *Stanley, on his expedition in Africa.*

Bananas are very nutritious – their calorific value is double that of meat. In Africa, as in other 'banana republics', plantains – green bananas – are cooked as a vegetable or, as in this Nigerian recipe, as chips.

Green bananas are sold in Indian and Caribbean shops.
Banana chips go very well with all types of pilav.

Plantains

These vary greatly in size. As a general rule allow 2 average plantains per person.

plantains
oil for frying

1 Peel the plantains and halve lengthways. Cut crossways into 1cm (½″) slices.
2 Heat sufficient oil to deep-fry, add the chipped plantains and fry for 4–5 minutes or until soft and light golden.
3 Remove with a slotted spoon, drain on kitchen paper and serve immediately.

Sughtoradz madzoon – garlic-yoghurt sauce

This very simple sauce is perhaps the most popular accompaniment for all kinds of rice or burghul pilavs in the Middle East, particularly in Turkey, Armenia and Iran.

Some people spoon the sauce over the pilav. I suggest you serve it as a side dish.

You can add 1–2 thinly sliced spring onions to the sauce.

300ml (½ pint) yoghurt
1 clove garlic, crushed
¼ teaspoon salt
½ teaspoon dried mint

Pour the yoghurt into a bowl. Mix the garlic and salt together and stir into the yoghurt. Sprinkle with the dried mint and serve.

Coban salatasi – shepherd's salad

A very popular salad from the mountains of Anatolia. Ideal with any meat dish.

4 tomatoes, thinly sliced
1 medium cucumber, peeled and thinly sliced
1 small onion, thinly sliced

1 small red pepper, thinly sliced
1 small green pepper, thinly sliced
2–3 spring onions, thinly sliced
1 Cos lettuce, washed and patted dry with kitchen paper

Dressing:
3 tablespoons olive oil
2 tablespoons lemon juice
2 teaspoons dried mint
½ teaspoon chilli pepper
1 teaspoon salt
½ teaspoon black pepper

Garnish:
2 tablespoons finely chopped parsley
3–4 radishes, thinly sliced

1 Place the sliced vegetables in a large salad bowl. Shred the lettuce leaves and add to the bowl.
2 Mix all the dressing ingredients together thoroughly and pour over the vegetables. Toss the salad well, sprinkle with the garnishes and serve.

Vzvar – dried fruit compote

This dried fruit compote is popular along the coastline of the Black Sea – Russia, Ukraine, Georgia, Turkey and Bulgaria. It is usually served at the early Christmas dinner celebrating the breaking of the fast. Serve it with any rice and burghul dishes, sprinkling the pilavs with this delicious mixture of fruit.

600ml (1 pint) water
250g (9oz) honey
5cm (2″) piece cinnamon stick
½ small lemon, sliced
⅛ teaspoon allspice
50g (2oz) of each of the following: dried apple slices, prunes, apricots, peaches, raisins or any other dried fruit
2–3 tablespoons brandy

1 Place the water and honey in a large saucepan and heat over a moderate heat until well blended.

2 Add the cinnamon stick, lemon slices, allspice and dried fruits and stir well. Cover the pan, lower the heat and simmer for 20 minutes or until the fruits are cooked, but still in whole pieces.

3 Remove from the heat, stir in the brandy, cover and leave to 'rest' for 5 minutes before serving.

Soba miso – buckwheat relish

Buckwheat is mixed with saké (rice wine) and miso (page 00) and used as a garnish for rice or vegetables.

75g (3oz) buckwheat
4 tablespoons saké
4–5 tablespoons miso

1 Toast the buckwheat in a large frying pan, turning and stirring regularly until well-browned.

2 Transfer to a bowl, add the saké and miso and mix thoroughly.

3 Use to garnish all types of plain or simple rice dishes.

Glossary

Tahina is a paste made from toasted and crushed sesame seeds. It is used in Middle Eastern cooking and can be purchased in small quantities from most health food shops, Middle Eastern and Indian stores.

Toasted nuts To toast almonds, walnuts, pine kernels, hazelnuts, peanuts etc. spread them out on silver foil, place under a grill or in the oven and cook until golden, turning at least once. Take care not to burn.

They can also be fried in a little oil, tossing and turning frequently until golden.

Pomegranate syrup This is the concentrated juice of the fruit and can be bought in some Middle Eastern and Greek shops.

Always dilute with a little water.

Sumac The dried, crushed berries of a species of the sumach tree. Has a sour, lemony flavour. Can be used in stews instead of lemon juice.

Should be available in some Middle Eastern stores.

Ghee is Indian butter which can be heated to a high temperature without burning. It is superior to ordinary butter and has a fragrance of its own.

Sold in all Indian shops.

Garam masala A mixture of ground spices used in the Indian and Pakistani cuisines.

Can be bought in most grocery stores.

Oils The oils suggested in this book are olive oil, corn oil, sunflower seed oil, sesame oil, peanut oil and soya bean oil. Of these perhaps only sesame oil and peanut oil are difficult to find.

Sesame oil is used in Far Eastern cooking and is extracted from toasted sesame seeds. It is used mainly for flavouring and can be found in Chinese shops.

Coconut is an important fruit-vegetable in the cuisine of the Far East, West Indies and Polynesia. It is used in several ways:
a) desiccated (dried and shredded),
b) milk – this is not the liquid inside the fruit, but the milky liquid

extracted from the grated flesh of a mature fruit. Tinned milk can be bought from Indian, Chinese and some health food shops. Always stir well before using.

c) creamed – this is sold in the form of white blocks and is, in reality, oil. It is used primarily in curries and stews as well as in sweet dishes.

Prepared sesame seeds You can buy these from Chinese and Japanese shops. If not available you can make your own.

225g (8oz) sesame seeds
1 teaspoon salt

Put the sesame seeds in a heavy frying pan over a moderate heat and brown, stirring constantly. Remove from the heat and stir the salt in thoroughly. Put the seeds in a blender and pulverise. Store in a tightly-lidded jar and use as instructed.

Miso – a paste made from cooked, fermented soy beans. It comes in different colours e.g. white, beige, brown and red and in varying degrees of saltiness. It should be available in Japanese shops and a few health food shops.

Drying mushrooms One of the great pastimes in Central and Eastern Europe is to gather mushrooms and then to either pickle or dry them for the forthcoming winter.

To dry first wipe them clean with a damp cloth, but do not wash. Remove the stems and peel the caps. Spread the caps on paper and leave them to dry for 3 days under the sun or in a warm place such as an airing cupboard. A quicker method is to place them in a very low oven for several hours, or until dry. To reconstitute, soak the mushrooms in warm water for 30 minutes before using. Chinese and Japanese dried mushrooms should also be soaked before use.

Soured cream Is also sold in shops as 'smetana'. It is not as tasty as the home-made version, but it will do for the recipes in this book. Natural yoghurt is a good substitute.

Salt pork (Petit salé de porc). This pickled pork can be purchased in jars. To prepare your own all you need to do is wash the pork (knuckles, cutlets, ears, fore-quarter flanks etc.) thoroughly in water. Transfer to a large pan.

Dissolve 450g (1lb) rock salt in 1 litre (1¾ pints) water. Bring to the boil, then leave to cool completely before pouring it over the meat. Cover the pan tightly. Leave for 3 days.

To serve, drain, boil in fresh water and serve as required.

Appendix 1

A few lines about other grains or grain products which are not used in this book, but some of which can be substituted for wheat, rice, rye or burghul.

Cous-cous – this is the rice/burghul of North Africa and is of Berber origin. It is made by steaming, drying and cracking grains of durum wheat (which has a lower gluten content than common wheat, but thrives in dry, semi-desert conditions and is widely grown in Mediterranean regions). It is usually served as a 'bed' for meat and vegetable dishes.

You can buy cous-cous grains from health and continental stores. All the tajine and cous-cous dishes of North Africa have these grains as their accompaniment. Cous-cous grains are also prepared from millet or buckwheat.

Sorghum (*Sorghum Vulgare*) – originated in North Africa about 3,000 BC. It was cultivated in Ancient Egypt. Today it is still popular throughout the region, as well as in India, China and the USA.

Grain-sorghum is a coarse grass which bears loose panicles containing up to 2,000 seeds per panicle. Types of cultivated grain-sorghum include kaffir, corn milo and durra (Africa), feteritas (Sudan), jowar, chalum shallu (India) and kaoliang (China).

Oats – native to Central Europe, oats are an important cereal of the temperate zone. It was developed about 2,500 BC in the Near East and Russia.

Oats arrived in Britain with the Roman legions and soon became a dietary staple of Northern Britain. The famed Scottish porridge is made from oats.

Oat groats are the whole oat grains with only the husks removed. They are pale yellow in colour, long and thin with a smooth, shiny surface. You can use oat groats just as wheat and rye, with most of the recipes in this book.

I have given below a simple oat groats recipe which can be used, with countless variations, to your heart's content. Make sure that the liquid/grain balance is right and remember that the cooking time is longer – approximately 50–60 minutes.

350g (12oz) whole oat groats
900ml (1½ pints) boiling water, stock or milk
1 teaspoon salt

Mix all the ingredients together in a large saucepan, cover and cook over a low heat for 50–60 minutes, stirring occasionally.

Triticale – this 'man-made' grain is a cross between wheat and rye, combining the high lysine content and strength of rye with the high protein content of wheat. Unfortunately it is as yet not easily available in Britain.

Polenta – similar to maize or cornmeal with a fine granular texture more like semolina. It is popular throughout Italy and the Balkans, particularly Romania where it is called 'mamaliga'.

Polenta is sometimes prepared with chestnut flour or buckwheat (Corsica).

Kishk – natural yoghurt and cracked wheat are fermented together, ground and dried under the sun or in the oven.

In the Balkans and Turkey this is called 'tarkana' (tarhonya) and is made by mixing flour, salt and egg. When dry it is cut into small pieces and added to stews and soups.

Semolina – Made from cereals e.g. millet, buckwheat, but mainly wheat. These grains are reduced to granules by coarse milling.

Appendix II Chemical composition of grains in %

Crops	Protein	Fats	Carbo-hydrates	Cellulose	Ash
Wheat	12	1.7	68.7	2.0	1.6
Rye	11	1.7	69.6	1.9	1.8
Barley	10.5	2.1	66.4	4.5	2.5
Oats	10.1	5.2	58.9	9.9	2.0
Corn	10	4.6	67.9	2.2	1.3
Buckwheat	11.3	2.7	58.3	11.3	2.4
Rice	6.6	1.9	62.3	10.2	5.1
Millet	9.9	2.9	72.9	3.2	2.5

Appendix III Essential amino acid content of whole grains

(as milligrams per 100g (3½oz) of edible portion)

Crop	Tryptophan	Threonine	Isoleucine	Leucine	Lysine	Methionine	Phenyl-alanine	Valine	Histidine
Wheat	164	383	577	892	365	203	657	616	271
Rye	137	448	515	813	494	191	571	631	276
Barley	160	433	545	889	433	184	661	643	239
Oats	183	770	733	1065	521	209	758	875	261
Corn	61	398	462	1296	288	186	454	510	206
Buckwheat	165	461	440	683	687	206	442	607	256
Rice: white	82	298	356	655	300	137	382	531	128
Rice: brown	81	294	352	646	296	135	377	524	126
Millet	248	456	635	1746	383	270	506	682	240

Bibliography

The Penguin Book of Zen Poetry ed. and tr. Lucien Stryk & Jak Ikemoto. Allen Lane, 1977
The Subtle Rose tr. R. R. Khawam. East–West Publications. London and The Hague, 1980
The Holy Bible Authorised and King James versions
The Art of Armenian Cooking Rose Baboian. Doubleday & Co Inc. NY 1964
The Manners and Customs of Modern Egyptians E. W. Lane, John Murray, 1860
The Book of the Dead R. O. Faulkner. The Limited Edition. Club NY 1972
The Unwritten Song W. R. Trask. Jonathan Cape, 1969
Ten Thousand Leaves Tr. Ian Hideo Levy, Princeton University Press USA, 1983
Penguin Book of Chinese Verse Tr. Robert Kotewall. Norman L. Smith, 1962
Ancient Records of Egypt 5 volumes. University of Chicago, 1906
Saidi Tr. Sir William Jones. ed. Muhammad Ali-Furughi. Tehran 1937
Chinese Fairytales and Folktales ed. Wolfram Eberhard. Kegan Paul, Trubner & Co., 1937
Three Centuries of Russian Poetry ed. Irina Zheleznova. Progress Publishers. Moscow, 1980

Index

Inca Wheat
(Chenopodium quinoa)